The Economics of Conformism

The Economics of Conformism

STEPHEN R.G. JONES

Basil Blackwell

First published 1984
Basil Blackwell Publisher Ltd
108 Cowley Road, Oxford OX4 1JF, UK

Basil Blackwell Inc.
432 Park Avenue South, Suite 1505,
New York, NY 10016, USA

British Library Cataloguing in Publication Data

Jones, Stephen R.G.
  The economics of conformism.
  1. Conformity
  I. Title
  153.8'54   HM291

  ISBN 0-631-13537-5

Typeset by MHL Typesetting Ltd, Coventry
Printed in Great Britain by Page Bros, Norwich Ltd

To my parents

Contents

Acknowledgements

It gives me great pleasure to record my gratitude for the help I have received throughout the course of work on this essay. I would like to acknowledge a special debt to three people. First, I am very grateful to George Akerlof, who supervised the Berkeley thesis upon which this book is based, for invaluable discussions, suggestions, and guidance. I would not have written this work without his help. I would also like to thank James Stock for countless conversations about the issues addressed in this book, and, indeed, for encouragement and stimulation throughout our entire graduate education. Many of my ideas were first heard by him, and his contribution is present, often in subtle ways, throughout this essay. Finally, I am indebted to Ellen Badone, both for moral support and for an intellectual exchange of ideas. To paraphrase Samuel Johnson, her thoughts made, for me, the new familiar and the familiar new.

I would also like to thank a number of other people who have assisted at different stages of this work. When the project was at an early stage, many people gave valuable guidance and constructive criticism: I would particularly like to thank Drew Fudenberg, Barry Ickes, James Pierce, Thomas Rothenberg, Lloyd Ulman, and Janet Yellen for their help. More recently, James Brander, Daniel Fusfeld, David Nickerson, and Thomas Schelling have provided useful comments on later versions of this study. In addition, I would like to thank my other teachers and colleagues at the University of California, Berkeley, and my present colleagues at the University of British Columbia, not least for creating a congenial and stimulating environment in which to work. I have presented some of the material in this essay at the University of California,

Berkeley, the University of British Columbia, Queen's University, the University of Toronto, and the University of Western Ontario, and I would like to extend my thanks to the participants in those seminars.

I would like to thank the University of British Columbia for excellent logistical support over the past few months, and in particular I would like to thank Teresa Patterson and Diana Kendall for excellent typing and word processing.

I also wish to record my gratitude for the financial support that I received during my graduate studies, when this book was initiated. I thank the University of Cambridge for a scholarship and the University of California, Berkeley, for a series of fellowships.

Finally, it is only appropriate, given my subject, that I conform to the tradition of claiming sole responsibility for all views expressed and for all errors that yet remain.

1

Introduction

There is an old joke which notes that, while the sociologist explains how people in society do not have any choices, the economist explains how these choices are made. Stated baldly, the ambitious aim that underlies this book is to offer a reconciliation and an integration of these two viewpoints. In general terms, of course, such a project is too much for one work, perhaps for one lifetime. The diversity of social phenomena within even a single culture, let alone the greater diversity across various types of social systems, belies any search for a simple yet universal explanation. Moreover, the range of theories to be found in economics and the other social sciences is very broad, and to find a general means of reconciliation is, to say the least, an exceedingly difficult task.

The particular purpose of this study is altogether more limited. My strategy is to proceed by means of an example, though it should be stressed at the outset that the example employed has much inherent interest and embodies a fair degree of generality. Furthermore, my treatment of this critical example indicates a more general methodology concerning the analysis of social behaviour, a methodology that, I believe, can indeed provide a way of reconciling the attitudes seen as so contradictory in the opening joke.

Social influence on behaviour can take many forms, and to some extent the works of anthropologists, social psychologists, and sociologists can be seen as documenting this variety. Moreover, the results of such social and societal pressures are typically characterized by a remarkable heterogeneity across groups and societies, so that conventional attitudes and behaviour in one context might be seen as unusual or idiosyncratic in another. Yet perhaps equally remarkable is the fact that, within each particular group or social context, opinions and actions tend to display a fair degree of homogeneity. Indeed, it is this very similarity that enables one to label one aspect of behaviour as conventional, given its context, and another in the same context as aberrant; furthermore, the definition of a group itself often hinges upon this homogeneity. For this reason, and on account of others that will be detailed, I regard social pressures to conform as a central instance of social influence. This example – conformism – will form the basis of the study that follows.

While this study is related to these various social sciences, it is equally important to understand its relation to economics. Since Adam Smith, the economic paradigm has been one of self-interested maximization – 'calculating avarice', in one writer's felicitous phrase. The strength of this postulate is well known, since it enables a level of precision and rigour in analysis unequalled in the social sciences. None the less, many alternative models of behaviour have been proposed, and it is useful briefly to contrast these various alternatives with the theory to be developed below.

Basically, two types of model have been advanced as alternatives to the standard economic paradigm. The first of these is individualistic, and amounts to a respecification of agents' objectives, retaining the individual as the central unit of analysis. In this vein, agents might not be seen as undeviatingly self-interested, and theories have been proposed where agents act altruistically (e.g. Vickery 1962, Nagel 1970, Arrow 1974, Becker 1974, 1976, Collard 1978, Sugden 1982, and Wintrobe 1983). In related, though logically distinct, work it has also been argued that agents might act according to some fundamental moral precepts, the outcomes of such behaviour not necessarily being coincident with those associated with altruism (e.g. Harsanyi 1955, Sen 1974, 1979, and Laffont 1975). In short, these approaches drop the postulate of 'avarice'. An alternative individualistic approach weakens the assumption of maximization, arguing that, for one reason or another, it is better to regard agents as following other behavioural strategies, sometimes labelled 'satisficing' (e.g. Simon 1957, Leibenstein 1976). This approach, then, removes the 'calculating' postulate, to the extent that this involves a conscious maximization. Of course, an individualistic alternative to the economic paradigm could also involve elements of any of these three models, since a person could be neither wholly calculating nor wholly avaricious.

The second type of alternative theory involves a more substantial departure from the economic paradigm, since it rejects the individual as the fundamental unit of analysis. For want of a better term, one might label this class of theories as 'holistic'. In general, Marxist analysis of class and the state illustrates this approach, where the individual choices underlying the 'actions' of collectives are of secondary importance: an outline of such a view is given in Giddens (1971). Similarly, some non-Marxist sociological theory has addressed issues relating to the 'collective consciousness', or to 'social currents', without specifying precisely the relation between such ideas and the actions taken by individual agents: the principal work in this vein is, of course, Durkheim (1938). In economics, too, various theories of collectives have been proposed, the early analysis of trade union behaviour being a prominent though not unrepresentative example (e.g. Dunlop 1944, Reder 1952, Rees 1962). Of course, such types of analysis have been criticized for their neglect of the public good problem (Olson 1965), and, rightly, many have been sceptical of conclusions derived from such models. Finally, a number of macroeconomic theories are implicitly holistic in form, since their microeconomic underpinnings are, at best, ill-specified.

In contrast to these many alternatives, the theory to be developed in this book remains squarely within the standard economic paradigm. That is, it maintains the individual as the unit of analysis, and, furthermore, it maintains the principle of self-interested maximization. The novelty of the model is straight-forward: it takes social influences upon behaviour directly into account. Hence, to the extent that actions are associated with social benefits or costs, the self-interested maximizer will take these perceived social rewards or penalties into account when deciding how to behave. Furthermore, the actions of this particular agent can, in turn, affect the social benefits and costs of various actions as perceived by the other agents. In this way, the outcomes achieved by a group of socially interdependent agents can reflect both the social influence each agent feels from the others and the social influence each agent exerts upon the other members of the group.

Thus, in keeping with the traditions of many social sciences other than economics, the role of social pressure is central; and, in keeping with the economic paradigm, such social factors have a role only to the extent that they affect the choices made by self-interested maximizing agents.[1]

The heart of this book consists of an examination of a particular example of social influence, that of conformism. Aside from the specific nature of these models, however, and the various conclusions that will be derived, it is useful briefly to examine some broad questions for which the theory to be developed is pertinent. I focus these introductory remarks on three issues.

The Nature and Origins of Normative Behaviour

For many years, economists have noted the possibility that social norms and customs can have an important effect upon behaviour. Indeed, such reference to the social context of economic actions can be traced back at least to Adam Smith (1759, 1776).[2] However, such acknowledgement of the role of normative behaviour tended, at best, to be of an informal nature. Customs were an appendage to economic theory proper, and they were typically adduced, by way of an afterthought, when a purely economic rationale seemed deficient.

Recently, a number of economic theorists have taken the idea of customary behaviour more seriously, and have attempted to develop theories in which custom is an integral aspect of the model. Akerlof (1980) proposed an economic theory of social custom with the property that, once the custom was established, considerations

---

[1] This is not to deny the possibility that there may be an interrelationship between social pressure and, for example, altruism or moral behaviour. Such a connection may be of prime importance in many instances, such as when behaviour according to a moral precept is associated with social approval. Indeed, it might even be argued that moral behaviour is learned through a process of social emulation. However, my point is that such a link is not necessary for social influence to play a role in determining behaviour, and, for simplicity, I neglect this possible extension.

[2] Skinner's (1974) introduction to *The Wealth of Nations* provides a valuable discussion of the relationship between these two works by Smith, stressing Smith's position that a social or ethical background was necessary for the effective operation of an economic system based on individualistic maximization.

of reputation made agents adhere to the custom even when, as would generally be the case, there were pecuniary gains to be had from violation.[3] Hence, cases may exist in which, when adherence to the custom is widespread, the reputation costs of violation outweigh these pecuniary gains, at the margin, thereby leading to a stable equilibrium in which the custom is upheld.

In addition, of course, such a model also admits of another stable equilibrium, in which, after violation has been so widespread that the reputation cost of further violation is minimal, agents neither believe in nor adhere to the custom. Akerlof used this type of model, in association with a custom concerning a fair wage, to construct a model of unemployment. In similar work, Hahn (1981) employed a social convention about the unemployed not under-cutting the wages of those employed to address the same type of issue; as he put it, 'I remind you again that workers are not peanuts' (Hahn 1981: 66). In a later paper, Akerlof (1982) built a model in which norms played a key role in determining the supply of effort, leading to a theory of labour contracts where workers supplied more effort than strictly required and where, in reciprocal 'gift exchange', the firm paid a wage in excess of the wage that would have cleared the labour market. More generally, Solow (1979a, 1980) has cogently argued that it seems sensible for any theory of the labour market to take such social factors into account.[4]

There have been two valuable accomplishments as a result of this work. First, it has shown how economic outcomes can be altered, often in a very important way, by the existence of a social conven-tion. Second, the way in which a social custom can persist, even in the presence of material incentives that favour violation, has been made clear. None the less, there remains an important sense in which such theories are incomplete, the heart of the problem being that the origins of such customs and norms have been left unspecified. As a result, although common sense is often a valuable guide, there remains a doubt that such conventions are rather

---

[3] The fact that a maverick who violates a social norm can typically make pecuniary gains by so doing is clear in, for example, Arrow (1972). The origins of this observation can be traced back at least as far as Becker's (1957) theory of discrimination.

[4] Such theories that take custom explicitly into account have not been limited solely to explaining the existence of unemployment, however. Akerlof (1983a) is an example in which such a modelling strategy is directed towards explaining the persistence of discrimination.

arbitrary.[5] To the extent that the microeconomic — or 'microsociological' — processes leading to the emergence of the custom are not specified, economic models that begin with a custom already in existence are only part of a complete theory.

There is a theory of the origins of social convention, of course, beginning, at least in recent times, with Schelling (1960). As developed by both philosophers (e.g. Lewis 1969, Ullmann-Margalit 1977) and more recently economists (e.g. Schelling 1978, Schotter 1981, Leibenstein 1982, 1984), the essence of this approach is that convention is a resolution of a 'coordination problem'.[6] In this way, customs and norms are the product of a stochastic, evolutionary-like process whereby a serendipitous outcome, once chanced upon, tends to persist.

Many important insights have emerged from this literature, especially concerning the incidence and nature of multiple equilibria. However, as with the economic theory that employed already existing conventions, this approach to the origin of customs seems to be incomplete. In particular, a constructive mechanism is lacking by which individual actions in a social context can produce a social norm. To paraphrase Quine's comments on language, if conventions exist, who did the convening?

The theory developed in this book seeks to remedy this incompleteness, proposing a particular constructive way in which, through the actions of self-interested agents in a social context, norms and traditions of behaviour can arise. As such, it is complementary to both approaches discussed above. It provides a microeconomic foundation for the origin of customary behaviour in labour markets, a foundation that adds a constructive element to the existing 'coordination problem' paradigm.

The Role of Custom in Economic Theory

In spite of the historical precedents mentioned above, it remains

---

[5] Much the same concern was expressed by Solow: 'I would be the first to admit that to allow yourself too free a hand with the stipulation of social conventions is to permit cheap "proof" of almost anything' (1979a: 348–49).

[6] This simple characterization is perhaps not quite fair to the subtleties of these various authors' arguments, though the key point is, I believe, valid.

true that the prevailing view among economists leaves little room for customs and norms. The papers that attempt to incorporate such social conventions explicitly into economic modelling, as cited above, amount to merely a handful, and are very much exceptions that confirm the rule. Part of the reason for this, of course, might merely be an interdisciplinary division of labour, with some types of problems being thought appropriate for economic analysis, while others are not. To the extent that social conventions and customs affect behaviour in economic contexts, of course, this fence-building rationale is open to question.

The principal reason why economists have paid little formal attention to norms of behaviour is more fundamental, however, and it stems from a particular view of the nature of such social processes. Perhaps the clearest recent statement of this position was given by Lucas:

> At some level of detail, there is no question that social convention and institutional structures affect these patterns [of behaviour we observe], but conventions and institutions do not simply come out of the blue, arbitrarily imposing themselves on individual agents. On the contrary, institutions and customs are designed precisely in order to aid in matching preferences and opportunities satisfactorily. [Lucas 1981: 4]

Hence, in this view customs are merely efficient solutions in disguise; and, to the extent that economists focus on the analysis of efficient equilibria, no need remains for an independent study of the role of custom.

It is true, as is argued above, that a theory based upon an arbitrary social convention is incomplete. Yet this need not imply that all custom is designed so as to generate efficient solutions. It is clear that most conventions and institutions are not, in any meaningful sense, 'designed'.[7] Rather, customs and traditions of behaviour typically arise independently of any agent's conscious attempts at design (see, e.g. Shils 1981.)[8] Furthermore, even in those

---

[7] As Popper wrote, 'Only a minority of social institutions are consciously designed, while the vast majority have just "grown", as the undesigned results of human actions' (Popper 1944: 122).

[8] Traditions may be invented, of course, as part of a broader manipulative political process. Yet it is clear that the outcomes of such political strategies, while important, do not encompass other than a small part of the behaviour we characterize as 'traditional'.

cases in which some types of institutions are designed – a company, a union, or a church, for example – the result usually reflects unanticipated and unintended social outcomes as much as conscious design. Hence, the observation that, were one designing a custom, one would design it to be efficient carries no particular implications for real-world social conventions, most of which are not – and perhaps could not be – so designed.

To some degree, however, the prevailing view of social customs need not hinge on the literal truth or falsehood of this 'design hypothesis'. Instead, reflecting a theme in the sociobiological literature (e.g. Wilson 1975, 1978, Barash 1979), it is argued that, for evolutionary reasons, only those customs most consistent with material survival – 'genetic fitness', in the sociobiologist's terms – will persist (e.g. Becker 1976).[9] Thus, simply because inefficient outcomes yield lower prospects of 'reproductive success' and hence tend to die out, in a literal sense, the efficiency of social conventions is rehabilitated without recourse to any particular model of how such conventions might arise.

In essence, this idea is a familiar one, resurrected by the language and techniques of sociobiology, since it amounts to a particular materialist version of the old functionalist view once dominant in anthropology.[10] Associated primarily with Radcliffe-Brown and Malinowski, the functionalist position held that all social conventions serve a positive function: 'The functionalist view of culture insists therefore upon the principle that in every type of civilization, every custom, material object, idea and belief fulfills some vital function...' (Malinowski 1926: 132). Yet, though still influential such a universal interpretation of functionalism fell into disrepute. Distinctions were made between 'manifest' and 'latent' functions

---

[9] Some would go even further, and direct this argument towards preferences themselves. For example, Michael and Becker write that 'if genetical natural selection and rational behavior reinforce each other in producing speedier and more efficient responses to changes in the environment, perhaps that common preference function has evolved over time by natural selection and rational choice as that preference function best adopted to human society' (1973: 392, n. 2).

[10] The social anthropoligist Leach has written as follows: 'The anthropologists have not solved all their problems in this area but they feel, with some justification, that, where human behaviour is concerned, most of the arguments now being put forward by the sociobiologists as if they were major scientific discoveries were effectively disposed of sometime around 1865' (Leach 1982: 100).

(Merton 1968, ch. III); a role was sought for the unintended consequences of social actions; and many other criticisms were advanced. Firth (1956) provides a wide-ranging critical survey.

More generally, it seems that such a functional position falls too easily into the trap of being an *ex post* rationalization. It is argued below that this problem is especially severe in the sociobiological (and economic) interpretation, where the function tends to be a material one, and where the logic is based on an incompletely specified evolutionary framework.[11] Manifestly, all extant behaviour patterns have persisted, so that they are 'consistent with survival', and it is unclear that much further insight than that can be drawn. It appears that many different types of custom, convention, and social organization satisfy this mild consistency condition, and that more structure is needed, beyond the simple evolutionary paradigm, to address this diversity in a serious way. As de Tocqueville remarked,

> I am tempted to believe that what we call necessary institutions are often no more than institutions to which we have grown accustomed, and that in matters of social constitution the field of possibilities is much more extensive than men living in their various societies are ready to imagine. [cited in Merton 1968: 490]

The present theory makes two points with regard to these issues. First, in providing a constructive way in which social customs can arise, it demonstrates the existence of an alternative both to the idea that customs are designed and to the idea that customs merely evolve in a purely stochastic manner. Second, when the theory is examined in a temporal context, the tradition model so generated entails a type of persistence in behaviour. Hence, if opportunities are changing, then present actions can reflect the 'matchings' of previous periods' opportunities and preferences, belying the purely materialist characterization implicit in the prevailing economic paradigm.[12] In this way, the theory reveals how, for a number of

---

[11] See Lumsden and Wilson (1981) for a more recent attempt to specify a 'coevolutionary process'. Valuable critiques of this book are given by Leach (1981) and Williams (1982).

[12] Tautologically, since my theory is based on the behaviour of self-interested maximizers, their actions reflect their opportunities and their preferences. When these preferences include considerations of conformism, however, no evolutionary-style materialist implication arises from such optimization. In particular, a 'stickiness' or persistence of behaviour, with regard to material opportunities, typically results, as will be made explicit in chapter 4 below.

reasons, the standard economic view of social custom and convention is unwarranted.

Economics and Sociology

Implicit in the opening sentence of this book was an opposition between the economic paradigm of choice and the sociological paradigm of social and societal constraints. As I said, a major purpose of the theory to be developed below is to illustrate how such a sharp contrast between the disciplines could be overcome. None the less, there remains an important distinction between the economic approach and that typically employed by sociologists, and it is this distinction that makes the subsequent analysis essentially economic.

If one were to select a single sociologist to whom one could attribute the view that 'people in society do not have any choices', it would probably be Durkheim. In *The Rules of Sociological Method* (1938), Durkheim proposed a complicated view of social behaviour based on societal pressures and constraints; and, to some degree, the theory to be presented below corresponds to his analysis of such social pressures. There is a key difference, however. Although the point is not explicit in Durkheim's own work, many later writers have interpreted his position as an assault on the individual as the basic unit of analysis. Thus, Giddens writes that 'the main burden of Durkheim's thesis is that *no* theory or analysis which begins from the 'individual' ... can successfully grasp the specific properties of *social* phenomena' (Giddens 1971: 87; italics in original).

To the extent that sociological analysis follows this non-individualistic paradigm, the theory presented below is clearly distinguished from sociology. The basic principle adopted is that of 'methodological individualism'. According to Popper, this view 'rightly insists that the "behaviour" and the "actions" of collectives, such as states or social groups, must be reduced to the behaviour and to the actions of human individuals' (Popper 1966: 91).[13] Thus, in trying to analyse social behaviour, it needs to be

---

[13]   See also Brodbeck (1968: section 4) for further discussion of holism and individualism in the social sciences.

demonstrated at each stage that the actions taken are, at an individual level, the best choices available to the agent. In this light, then, in so far as social pressures play a key role in affecting behaviour, they do so solely to the extent that they alter the actions taken by individuals. Further, these social pressures themselves arise as a result of individual choices and interactions, and exist only through individual actions making these pressures and influences concrete.

It is worth stressing what adopting a methodological individualist approach does *not* imply. It does not mean that people behave in the same way in a group context as they would in isolation. It does not mean that the 'behaviour' of society is a simple aggregation across the behaviour patterns of individuals. And it does not mean that there is no role for, as examples, class consciousness, patriotism, or the presence of a Protestant 'work ethic'. Rather, the methodological individualist position leaves a potential role for all of these various influences, and for others, provided it can be demonstrated that they both arise from and affect the decisions made by individual agents.

Thus, my use of the individual as the basic unit of analysis distinguishes this work from much of the sociological literature. Further, it enables a direct use of the tools of optimizing behaviour that economists have developed; in particular, I employ the technique of utility maximization. Since social pressures only arise from and only affect individual choices, the economic theory of choice can be used to analyse these social issues. In this way, an individualistic theory of social custom can be developed, based upon the idea of conformism.

Outline

In presenting an economic theory of conformism, I have chosen to focus on one particular example: conformism as displayed in a workplace context. There are two separate reasons for doing this. First, the specificity of an example makes the exposition simple and clear, whereas the theory might be obfuscating in the abstract. Second, the example chosen has much inherent interest. As mentioned above, many writers have addressed the role of custom in affecting labour market behaviour, and our work can be seen in that tradition. Moreover, the particular conclusions this example yields have considerable importance for the functioning of firms and labour markets.

The book proceeds as follows. In chapter 2, I draw upon some of the social psychology and sociology literature to argue that conformism is both pervasive and, to the economist theorist at least, novel. Specific examples are given of conformity in workplaces and elsewhere; and, in addition to a wide variety of informal evidence, one particular datum from the classic Hawthorne studies is considered to enable a more formal treatment of the nature of conformity. The basic theory is presented in chapter 3, where a detailed characterization of individual decision-making in a social environment is presented, and where the properties of the model and various extensions are examined. The theory is given a temporal structure − that of overlapping generations − in chapter 4, which leads to a model of tradition, the implications of which, both particular and general, are detailed. This framework is then taken a step further in chapter 5, leading to a model of the internalization of values in a process of socialization. Finally, chapter 6 reviews some broader implications of the theory, and proposes some areas for future research.

2

The Nature of Conformism

To some extent, the present work is an unusual enterprise in economics. While its techniques and its theoretical paradigm are quite standard, from the viewpoint of an economist, the issues that it addresses and, indeed, the primitives that guide the theory are rather novel. The purpose of this chapter is to examine the nature of these fundamental issues: to seek to establish the terms of references in attempting an economic analysis of social influence.

The strategy employed is to detail some of the work performed by social psychologists and sociologists in the study of conformism. This body of research both documents conformity and, more importantly, reveals the types of social psychological mechanisms that underlie such behaviour. Yet, it should be stressed at the outset, the aims of this examination differ somewhat from those implicit in past surveys of such literature.[1]

First, I wish to establish the extent to which processes of social influence – especially conformism – are general characteristics of behaviour, rather than just being, for example, particular artefacts of the social psychologist's laboratory. Clearly, unless conformism is reasonably characterized as a general trait, it should not form the basis of an economic theory with some alleged generality. Second – and this is the principal point of departure of the present treatment, relative to past analyses – I shall seek to examine whether it makes sense for the economic theorist to take conformism as, in a

---

[1] Surveys of the social psychological literature on conformism are provided by, among many others, Jones and Gerard (1967), Kiesler and Kiesler (1969), Gerard and Conolley (1972), and Aronson (1980).

manner to be made precise below, a primitive of the model. In previous economic work, various social phenomena have been regarded as the results of strictly material choices made by people, with these choices often being quite complicated and sophisticated. That is, social behaviour has been seen as an endogenous outcome arising from particular economic circumstances. The present focus is different, however, in that I wish to study whether such conformism can rather be taken as a primitive, even allowing for the fact that people may implement quite sophisticated economic strategies.

Jane Austen remarked towards the end of *Northanger Abbey* that the reader could infer the imminent happy conclusion of the book from the 'tell-tale compression of the pages'. Perhaps the present tell-tale thickness of the text to follow similarly reveals our answers to these two questions. It is argued that conformism is a phenomenon of considerable generality, evidenced in workplaces, schools, the military, the social psychology laboratory, and elsewhere. It is further argued that, to an important degree, it is misleading to regard such conformity purely as a strategic response to material economic circumstances; rather, conformist behaviour obtains in many situations where the purely economic incentive to conform is minimal or even negative. Accordingly, such conformism poses a new issue for economic theory to address, a challenge which is taken up in subsequent chapters.

The examination of this evidence about conformist behaviour is organized as follows. I shall first consider a variety of examples of conformism, as exhibited in many different settings. I concentrate on instances of social influence and conformist behaviour in workplaces, both because this case has a particular relevance for the economist and because the theory will use social interactions in a workplace as its example. However, while indicating the potential generality of conformism, such examples suffer from being imprecise observations of real-world events, whereas in reality a wide range of possible explanations could account for the observed actions. Hence, in order to focus on the nature of such behaviour I shall then examine some experimental data from social psychology; these enable a purging of extraneous influences and incentives and reveal the sense in which conformism can be taken as a primitive by the economist. Finally, given this logical framework, I return to the case of workplace behaviour, examining one particular datum from a classic study to see whether, allowing for sophisticated economic strategies, conformist behaviour still has an independent role to play.

The Generality of Conformism

It is an ill-defined task, in a formal sense, to assess the degree to which conformism is a general characteristic of social behaviour. There is no natural choice of measure to assess the importance of such a social process, and although situations can be envisaged and experiments designed to address such issues, a precise quantitative assessment remains difficult. It does not follow, however, that because a social process is hard to quantify it must be unimportant, any more than difficulties in measuring such factors as love, trust, or loyalty would lead one to conclude that these aspects of life are of secondary concern. Thus, in a sense, the problem of assessing the role of conformism is just one instance of the more general problem of evaluating how well a model – any model – fits the world. Ultimately, our judgement of a model is a judgement about its plausibility.

I shall proceed by considering three famous examples of social influence: attitudes and behaviour in a college environment, in the US Army during the Second World War, and in some small-group workplace situations. Before this, however, two points should be noted.

First, the idea of conformism is both simple and familiar. The phenomenon of conformity is mundane precisely because it accords closely with our everyday experience, our commonplace behaviour. Thus, to cite just a few examples, the teenager experiments with illicit drugs, conforming to the behaviour patterns of his or her peers at high school; the prospective undergraduate is likely to learn that the 'pressures to conform' are greater at college A than at college B; the new member of a college society adopts the attitudes of the more senior members; and so on. Further, commonplace phrases such as 'peer pressure', 'regression to the mean', and 'go with the flow' attest to the importance of conformity in daily life. As the saying goes, 'When in Rome, do as the Romans do.'

Yet there is another side to all of this, the implications of which belie the 'mundane' characterization of conformity. Precisely to the extent that such behaviour pervades our social lives, it lies at the heart of social analysis. The sociologist Robert K. Merton wrote:

> The mesh of expectancies constituting every social order is sustained
> by the modal behavior of its members representing conformity to the
> established, though perhaps secularly changing, culture patterns. It
> is, in fact, only because behavior is typically oriented toward the
> basic values of the society that we may speak of a human aggregate
> as comprising a society. [Merton 1968: 195]

From the process of socialization as a child through the pressures
from the myriad of groups to which most people belong, conformity
seems to lie at the centre of much tradition, custom, and culture. As
the social anthropologist Edmund Leach put it,

> We do not live exactly as our parents lived but whatever we do now
> is only a modification of what was done before. It could hardly be
> otherwise. Very little of our public behaviour is innate; most of us
> have only very limited creative originality. We act as we do because,
> one way or another, we have learned from others that that is the way
> we ought to behave. [Leach 1982: 128]

Paradoxically, then, though conformism is commonplace, it is also
fundamental.

The first of the three examples is drawn from a study conducted
among the students at Bennington College in the eastern United
States during the late 1930s (Newcomb 1943). Coming from pre-
dominantly conservative families, these students tended, as freshmen, to share the conservative attitudes of their parents.[2] However,
as Newcomb detailed, through a process of extended social interaction with more progressive older students and faculty, these
'conservative freshmen' became 'liberal seniors'.

This conformity of the young to the old was recorded in two ways.
First, a series of standardized tests of attitudes − about unions,
social security, the regulation of monopolies, and so on − was ad-

---

[2] It is interesting to note that this intergenerational transmission of attitudes, a commonplace in everyday life, can be seen within the context of the theory below and its underlying
social psychology; see, e.g., Jones and Gerard (1967: ch. 3).

ministered to several classes over several consecutive years, with Newcomb finding that each class became more liberal, on the average, with each year spent at Bennington.[3] Second, the nature of the qualitative response Newcomb observed to unique issues, such as the Spanish Civil War, was interpreted as revealing that the students had adopted a more progressive philosophy, rather than just conforming by rote to pressure on particular issues.

It is worth noting that, while the progressive students at Bennington were very popular, tending to occupy positions of leadership, the more conservative students were, for the most part, socially isolated. This suggests that there were social rewards for the young to gain by conforming to the attitudes of the older students.

Finally, in a follow-up study conducted 25 years later, it was found that opinions had by and large remained as they had been when the students had graduated from Bennington (Newcomb, Koenig, Flacks, and Warwick 1967). This suggests that such attitude change tended to be a persistent and fundamental alteration in views, rather than, for example, merely transitory compliance.

Another example of this adoption of the attitudes of respected others, in a social setting, comes from the study *The American Soldier* (Stouffer et al. 1949, vols I and II), where a wide range of hypotheses about interpersonal interaction was examined empirically, using detailed evidence collected during the Second World War. As a result of high personnel turnover among combat troops, three group situations were available for study: (i) inexperienced troops in outfits consisting wholly of their own kind; (ii) inexperienced troops, sent in as replacements, in outfits comprising combat veterans; and (iii) veterans among their peers. In a wide variety of questions, there were systematic differences in the responses given by these three groups. For example, while 45 per cent of the inexperienced troops were ready to 'get into an actual battle zone', this was true of only 28 per cent of the replacements and 15 per cent of the veterans (vol. II: 248).

There were also objective measures of the importance of group context. In companies where veterans had high rates of non-battle

---

[3] These tests were administered to one class for four consecutive years, to two classes for three consecutive years, and to two classes for two consecutive years.

casualties, non-veterans also had high rates, with a correlation coefficient of $+0.80$ (vol. II: 27).[4,5] Thus, although new recruits might initially be thought similar, the effect of being placed in a group with other green troops, compared with being placed in a group of veterans, was to produce substantial differences in both attitudes and performance. As one of the authors of the study wrote, 'to some extent the replacements took over the attitudes of the combat veterans around them, whose views on combat would have for them high prestige' (vol. II: 250). To some degree, then, conformism is the sincerest form of flattery, reflecting a desire to adopt the attitudes of others with high prestige, and to be accepted as a member of their group.[6]

Our final example comes from a famous series of studies of workplace behaviour undertaken at the Hawthorne plant of the Western Electric Company in Chicago, Illinois, between 1927 and 1932 (Roethlisberger and Dickson 1939).[7] Of these many studies, we concentrate upon the last, which took place in the 'Bank Wiring Observation Room' over a seven-month period ending, as a result of a shortage of funds owing to the Great Depression, in May 1932. The study concerned the behaviour of 14 men who worked in a group, wiring, soldering, and inspecting 'banks' of electrical terminals used in telephone equipment, and who were paid wages that depended, in a rather complicated way, upon the average output of the group.

The main conclusion of this research was that, to a degree that seemed to surprise the investigators, the men conformed to a 'norm'

---

[4] The data from *The American Soldier* presented here are based upon the following sample sizes: 427 veterans, 406 replacements, and 7493 inexperienced division members for the attitude survey; and 361 veteran noncoms, 704 veteran privates, and 532 non-veteran privates for the non-battle casualty data (Stouffer et al. 1949, vol. II: 248 and 27, respectively).

[5] The statistic 'non-battle casualties' was used in the study as the best proxy for the overall performance of a unit. As the authors of the study wrote, 'After a laborious study, the research team arrived at the conclusion that the only index, at the company level, which could be defended as both reliable and meaningful would be the nonbattle casualty rate' (Stouffer et al. 1949, vol. II: 6).

[6] There may be a parallel here between these group pressures and the work of Hirschman (1970). Through *loyalty* to the group, an agent may conform; he or she may persuade others to conform by *voice*; and, if conformity is not achieved, he or she may *exit*.

[7] Other accounts and discussions of these Hawthorne studies are given by Mayo (1933, 1945), Whitehead (1938), and Homans (1951). There is now a vast literature on these studies, and some notable retrospective analyses are given by Landsberger (1958), Dickson and Roethlisberger (1966), and Cass and Zimmer (1975).

of output, which involved making about 6600 connections each day. According to Elton Mayo,

> the working group as a whole actually determined the output of individual workers by reference to a standard, pre-determined but never clearly stated, that represented the group conception of a fair day's work. This standard was rarely, if ever, in accord with the standards of the efficiency engineers. [Mayo 1945: 79]

In an exhaustive survey of possible explanations of this behaviour, which incidentally was noted by the researchers as negating the intentions of the complicated incentive scheme, Roethlisberger and Dickson concluded that 'Their [the men's] concept of a day's work did not represent a personally calculated equilibrium between work and monetary return' (1939: 416).

This conformism was achieved through a process of social interactions in the workplace. Membership in, and loyalty to, two loosely defined cliques within the Observation Room encouraged a worker's self-motivation to conform. Verbal jibes, such as calling the faster workers 'Speed King', 'Lightning', and 'Cyclone', and physical gestures such as 'binging' (hitting another man as hard as possible on the upper arm) added to these pressures. Thus, the evidence from the Bank Wiring Observation Room study supports two claims: first, that the workers did appear to care about one another's actions *per se*; and second, that, as a result, they behaved in a conformist manner.[8]

---

[8] To many people, the most important aspect of these studies was the discovery of the so-called 'Hawthorne effect', whereby consciousness of being studied coupled with a desire to please the investigators made for unusual and even bizarre results. For example, in some early experiments on the interrelation of the intensity of lighting and the level of productivity — the illumination experiments — it was found that the young women involved continued to produce at their former high level even when they were essentially working in moonlight (Roethlisberger and Dickson 1939: 17). Similarly, in the 'Relay Assembly Test Room', no simple relation between working conditions and output was found. Rather, the workers' awareness of the special nature of their situation seemed to have its own effect, confounding the changes the investigators made in the independent variable under study.

Apart from being a salutory warning about the hazards of experimentation, we take the 'Hawthorne effect' as a sign that the mental and social orientations of workers can be critical in affecting output. It is therefore not an end in itself; no one seriously suggests, for example, that English factory managers should institute endless series of experiments, hoping to induce a sequence of positive Hawthorne effects! Rather, the conclusion to be inferred is that such worker orientations, in a social context, need further study, as was done to some degree in the later Hawthorne studies and is being done, on a more theoretical plane, in this essay.

Finally, it is important to note that this type of conformist behaviour is typical of many workplaces, as detailed in a wealth of other studies. For example, Whyte (1955) reported evidence from a large machine shop where, of 84 experienced men subdivided into smaller cliques, only 9 were classified as 'ratebusters' by Dalton, a graduate student investigator who worked at the shop. Seashore (1954) studied 228 different work groups, ranging in size from 5 to 50 members, and established that group cohesion could be associated with either high or low productivity. In his study of the 'cash posters', Homans (1953, 1954) emphasized how group interactions affected the effort and output of the workers, first when pressure was put on the faster workers to slow down, and later when sentiment for co-workers may have induced greater effort than would otherwise have been the case. (On this latter phenomenon, see Akerlof 1982.) More recently, in a study comparing British and Japanese factories, Dore reported the response to a survey that, among other questions, asked workers whether they could work at their own pace: 78 per cent of the British engineering sample said that they could, compared with only 25 per cent of the Hitachi group (Dore 1973: 231). It was argued that, even when adjusted for some technological constraints, this difference showed significant cultural and organizational contrasts. The 'groupishness' of the Japanese, and their greater tendency towards conformity, were key characteristics highlighted in Dore's meticulous study.[9,10]

Perhaps the most convincing evidence of the importance of such social pressures in workplaces comes from the recent work of industrial psychologists and organizational behaviour specialists. While many general theories of motivation have been proposed, two of the most dominant views in 'implicit personality theory' used to be 'Theory X' and 'Theory Y'. According to McGregor (1960), Theory X managers begin with the premise that workers are lazy, given to shirking, and must be closely supervised and directed. In contrast, a

---

[9] Without overemphasizing the point, I suggest that such differences in conformism may be related, in a complicated way, to differences in economic performance. Gordon (1982) proposed one such analysis among countries, based on cultural differences. See also the discussion of a Nissan plant in the United States in chapter 4, pp. 79–80 below.

[10] Other useful discussions of the Japanese experience include Clark (1979), Cole (1979), and White and Trevor (1983). For a related examination of these issues, see Leibenstein (1984).

Theory Y manager starts with the beliefs that workers are self-directed, that they enjoy meaningful work, and that they like to have responsibility and independence. Of course, such stereotypes are at best an approximation, at worst a misleading caricature. What is more important is that, by and large, such individualistic approaches have declined in importance in the analysis of organizational behaviour.

In their place, many researchers and consultants in the field have given much greater weight to the role of group norms, and to factors affecting conformity to those norms. Thus, for example, Bass and Barrett (1972), in a standard text on industrial psychology, suggest that group cohesiveness can have an important effect upon productivity, and are led to advocate participative techniques as a consequence.[11] Similarly, Blake and Mouton (1981) have proposed a 'social dynamics' approach to productivity, stressing the key role played by groups and by pressures to conform. In perhaps the clearest statement of all, Ouchi (1981) has proposed a 'Theory Z', his alternative to Theories X and Y, based on social pressures in a workplace. As he argues,

> What we care about most is what our peers think about us ... More than hierarchical control, pay, or promotion, it is our group memberships that influence our behavior. There are daily examples of the tremendous power group memberships can exert upon people to the extent of changing their religious beliefs, their attitudes towards work, and even their self-image ... It is not external evaluation or rewards that matter in such a setting [the workplace], it is the intimate, subtle and complex evaluation by one's peers − people who cannot be fooled − which is paramount. [Ouchi 1981: 25]

It seems, then, that there are good reasons why we will select conformism in workplaces as our canonical example.

Problems with the Evidence

The principal difficulty with such evidence is that, while it seems

---

[11] See also Maier (1973), McCormick and Tiffin (1974), Landy and Trumbo (1976), and Ribeaux and Poppleton (1978) for similar discussions.

plausible to infer the presence of social pressures to conform, a plethora of factors affecting behaviour make it hard to rule out other explanations. In particular, from the viewpoint of an economist, one cannot easily reject an analysis based primarily upon information and incentives, excluding socially based incentives to conform. For example, to the extent that the Bennington students were presented with new information – cogent arguments for a liberal position, say, which they had never heard from their parents – the changes in their behaviour might simply reflect rational acquisition and processing of this data. Similarly, the new recruit in the US Army might very reasonably reckon to learn how to get by in unfamiliar circumstances simply by copying the veterans' actions and attitudes: they certainly knew more than the raw recruit about 'actual battle zones', for example. Finally, the evidence from workplaces can be questioned since, as a rule, the economic incentives that the workers faced have not been accounted for with great care, so such conformist tendencies could be seen as strategic endogenous responses to economic opportunities in a working group context.

The existence of these problems in interpreting real-world evidence does not vitiate the social psychological reading, of course, any more than it undermines a purely economic rationale. Like the famous tale of a group of blind people, each examining one part of an elephant, the social psychologist may be seeing one aspect of the whole, the economist another. Or, to change the image, reactions to such case-studies are akin to responses to Rorschach ink blots. One person's social influence is another person's strategic response to an interdependent incentive structure; and perhaps, like an optical illusion, one can sometimes see one aspect, sometimes another, and sometimes just an ink blot.

There seem to be two ways out of this dilemma, each of which has been used to some degree by social psychologists and others. The first is to collect more and better evidence in these real-world situations. Thus, one can attempt to allow for the role of information or incentives, and one can enquire directly as to motivation by, for example, the use of interviews, though problems certainly exist in interpreting such data. The second technique is to depart from the uncontrolled context of daily behaviour, and to construct social psychological experiments, thereby abstracting from as many extraneous forces as possible. Such studies enable a precise analysis, for example, of the types of social pressure that can lead to conformism, though, of course, it has then to be established that such pressures are indeed critical in contexts outside the laboratory. Since this type of breakdown of the factors affecting conformism is central to this study, we will now briefly examine some of this experimental work.

Experimental Social Psychology

From the early work of Allport (1920) and Moore (1921), social psychologists have employed a great variety of experimental designs in evaluating the nature and importance of conformism. Sherif (1935, 1936) introduced a study based on 'autokinetic illusion', the tendency for a stationary light source in an otherwise completely darkened room to appear to move, assessing the convergence of individual opinions to a group consensus or norm. Festinger and his colleagues (Bach 1951, Festinger and Thibaut 1951, Schachter 1951, and Gerard 1954) employed a group discussion procedure, evaluating the extent to which attitudes about issues such as the plight of 'Johnny Rocco', a fictitious juvenile delinquent, were affected by group pressures. The classic experiment, however, was that conducted by Asch (1951, 1952, 1956), and it is on this research, and its successors, that we will focus.

In the Asch study, a subject was asked to match the length of a sample line with that of one of three comparison lines. Each subject was placed in a group of six to eight people, who announced their answers in a pre-established order, with the subject answering next to the last. All of the other group members, however, were confederates of the researcher, and they had previously been instructed to respond incorrectly − all giving the same wrong answer − on certain trials. Hence, on these critical trials, the subject had a clear, though difficult, choice: to accept the evidence of his senses, and give the correct but non-conformist answer; or to accede to the unanimous opinion of a group of his − apparent − peers and give the incorrect, conformist answer.[12] Of 123 subjects tested, 75 per

[12] The fact that there were no explicit rewards or penalties in Asch's experiment should not be taken as a sign that the subjects' choices were a matter of indifference for them. Indeed, the mental anguish that many of the subjects displayed suggests quite the opposite: that the

cent agreed with the majority to some degree. Further, whereas in a control group mistakes were made less than 1 per cent of the time, under group pressure 'mistakes' were made in 36.8 per cent of the critical trials.

There seem to be two possible explanations of Asch's results. The first is that, in addition to his own judgement, the subject is employing the other group members' estimates as information. He employs the behaviour of the others – in this case, their estimates of the length of a line – as a means of evaluating and thereby modifying his own behaviour. The alternative explanation is that, mindful of the impression he is making on the other group members, who he might presume expect a conforming response, the subject agrees with their estimate. He is concerned about acceptance by the group, and about a possible loss of status – being thought a fool – should he disagree.

Subsequent to the Asch study, a good deal of research sought to highlight the relative strength of these two effects. A number of studies (e.g. Asch 1952, Garard and Greenbaum 1962) sought to introduce stimulus ambiguity, testing the extent to which, as the subject's judgemental problem became more difficult, he or she relied to a greater degree on the estimates of others. Further, by affecting the degree of expertise attributed by the subject to the group, relative to himself or herself – by giving bogus feedback about performance, for example, or giving prior information on expert status – several studies demonstrated the presence and sensitivity of the information dependence (see, e.g., Goldberg and Lubin 1958, Mausner 1954a, 1954b, Snyder, Mischel, and Lott 1960, and Gerard 1961).

In addition to these studies, which revealed the role of information in various forms, several researchers also devised techniques to examine the importance of direct social pressure. Deutsch and Gerard (1955) proposed a refinement of the Asch technique, comparing the responses of subjects when physically isolated and

---

dilemma with which they were faced was a serious one. All through life, people have to make correct judgements about their physical environment while at the same time interacting with other people, which often involves living up to others' expectations. The subjects in Asch's study had these two important aspects of life in conflict, and their evident difficulties in resolving such a problem implied that, while no material incentives were offered, the implicit rewards and penalties were substantial.

anonymous with their responses in a public, face-to-face, group context. The authors argued that, to the extent that conformity persisted in the case of isolation, it reflected information dependence. Further, to the extent that greater conformity might be evidenced in the face-to-face setting, this difference revealed an additional effect which could be attributed to social pressure.[13] Their findings, that on the average subjects conformed in 7.08 of 24 critical trials in the public setting and in 5.92 of 24 trials in the case of anonymity, provided support for the presence of both effects. In a similar vein, Mouton, Blake, and Olmsted (1956) utilized the subjects' anonymity, in this case asking them to judge the number of metronome clicks heard, and found greater conformity in the public setting, when the subject could be identified with his or her own judgement, and when the capacity for direct social pressure existed. It seems, then, that both types of appraisal were probably present, with resultant behaviour being both informationally based and cognizant of the social effects of nonconformity.

A recent study (Ross, Bierbrauer, and Hoffman 1976) illustrated this mixed conclusion clearly. In this experiment, which closely resembled that of Asch in structure, conformity was initially seen in 26 per cent of the critical trials. However, when the subject was provided with a plausible reason why the group apparently gave incorrect answers − based on a complicated payoff structure which made it seem as though the others were gambling, and which made it plausible that they did not think their answers correct − conformity fell to 18 per cent of the trials. In this instance, the subject could attribute the others' behaviour to this external reason, thereby reducing the informational conflict he or she faced. Further, when it was made clear to both the subject and the group that the subject did not share their good reason for gambling − in fact, when it was made common knowledge − the incidence of conformity fell to only 10 per cent. That is, when the nonconformist behaviour of the subject could be attributed to some external cause, the degree of normative social influence fell.

---

[13] Even in the case of isolation, of course, the subject might know that the researcher was watching for potentially wrong answers. Since this effect was also present in the face-to-face context, however, the conclusion about the differential conformism in the two situations remains valid.

In summary, the evidence from experimental social psychology documents the presence of conformity in many carefully controlled settings. Further, it suggests that there are two elements, strategic and informational factors and normative social factors, that underlie such outcomes. In many experiments both elements were found to be present, although, as many writers have emphasized, their relative importance seems to depend critically on context. Accordingly, it is appropriate briefly to re-examine our examples of conformism in the light of these experimental results.

The Examples Reconsidered

Newcomb's (1943) study was sufficiently detailed and painstaking that it is possible to distinguish between informationally based conformism and conformism that arose as a result of social pressure. As a general result, it seems that evidence can be found in the book suggesting both types of motivation. For our purpose, however, it suffices to note that a theory built upon strategic or information-related behaviour misses a large part of his findings, so that a conventional economic analysis would be, at best, incomplete.

We noted above that, while the liberal seniors tended to be among the most popular students at Bennington, the few who had retained their conservative views were typically socially isolated, suggesting the presence of social rewards to conformity. Such an interpretation is further supported by, for example, the comments given by students in interviews, some of which we now quote:

> 'It's very simple. I was so anxious to be accepted that I acquired the political complexion of the community here.'|[Newcomb 1942: 132]
> 'I accepted liberal attitudes here because I had always secretly felt that my family was narrow and intolerant, and because such attitudes had prestige value.' |[p.137]|
> 'It didn't take me long to see that liberal attitudes had prestige value...I became liberal at first because of its prestige value; I remain so because the problems around which my liberalism centers are important. What I want now is to be effective in solving the problems.' [p.136]

Interestingly, then, such social rewards to conforming did not just generate transitory compliance, though even such compliance is of interest, of course. Rather, these processes produced deep-rooted changes in attitudes − the internalization of these values − which persisted well beyond the students' years at Bennington.

In a similar way, the detailed evidence in *The American Soldier* suggests that both types of conformism were present. Objectively, the new recruit may have been able to learn by emulating the more senior soldiers; but, in addition, there were social benefits, supplementing any material gains, that enhanced the tendency toward conformism. As Merton wrote, discussing this particular evidence:

> The function of conformity is acceptance by the group, just as progressive acceptance by the group reinforces the tendency toward conformity. And the values of these 'significant others' constitute the mirrors in which individuals see their self-image and reach self-appraisals. Applied to the specific case in hand, the significant others in the membership-group are similarly inexperienced men for the green soldier in the green outfit, whereas for the replacement, the significant others are experienced veterans, with their distinctive sets of values and sentiments. [Merton 1968: 308]

Although the replacement might learn by imitation, then, the rewards to such behaviour were, in an immediate sense, social rather than material.

Finally, in reviewing the evidence from the Hawthorne studies, it is unclear exactly how a purely informational reading of the workers' actions could be developed. One can, however, interpret the learning-by-imitation analysis of conformism more generally as an instance of strategic economic behaviour, in which case the relevant question is whether one can account for the Hawthorne evidence in this broad economic framework. Since this is clearly a question of some importance, I propose a rather detailed analysis of the issue, using the well documented case of the workers in the Bank Wiring Observation Room. Rather surprisingly, given the problems generally encountered in the interpretation of non-experimental data, we will find that such evidence is capable of providing a fairly clear answer to our question.

The Hawthorne Puzzle

One particular observation from the Hawthorne study will be used to permit a precise, formal examination of the workers' behaviour. This observation is that, in the context of a particular wage schedule, implemented by a non-competitive firm,[14] workers put pressure on the slower members of the working group to speed up, *and* on the faster members of the group to slow down. Under the supposition that each worker cares only about his or her wage and disutility of effort, such 'two-sided pressure' is difficult, although not impossible, to explain. Yet this difficulty has an inherent interest, and the fact that a straightforward interpretation cannot explain this two-sided pressure constitutes the 'Hawthorne puzzle'. The resolution of this apparent problem is trivial, of course, once the role of conformity is recognized, and the theory in chapter 3, aside from its other purposes, can be seen as an explicit model of the type of behaviour involved in the Bank Wiring Observation Room.

In their summary of the sentiments displayed by the workers in the Hawthorne plant Bank Wiring Observation Room, Roethlisberger and Dickson listed, among others, the following:

(1) You should not turn out too much work. If you do, you are a 'ratebuster'.
(2) You should not turn out too little work. If you do, you are a 'chiseler'. [Roethlisberger and Dickson 1939: 522].

That is, social forces within the working group were of this two-sided nature, with both potential 'ratebusters' and potential 'chiselers' being pressured to move towards the group norm, which, as noted above, was about 6600 connections a day (Roethlisberger and Dickson 1939: 413).[15] Can this two-sided pressure be explained in a standard economic model?

The most natural such model to adopt supposes that each worker maximizes an additively separable utility function of the form:

---

[14] Such a description would naturally apply to the Western Electric Company.

[15] In light of this vocabulary, the reader might legitimately wonder whether the workers' behaviour was not a strategic response to material circumstances. Later, I develop a precise argument that it was *not*, and also discuss why these apparent attitudes were evidenced.

$$U^i(W_i, e_i) = V(W_i) - C_i(e_i) \tag{2.1}$$

where W_i and e_i are the ith worker's wage and effort, respectively. Here, the first term represents the utility of wage income, where $V' > 0$, $V'' \leqslant 0$. The second, idiosyncratic, term represents the disutility of effort of agent i, with $C_i' > 0$, $C_i'' \geqslant 0$ for each i. This specification guarantees that leisure is a normal good,[16] and it nests many particular functional forms as special cases.

Since there cannot be any interdependence of effort levels through the second term of (2.1), we can concentrate upon the wage schedule. In the Hawthorne plant itself, the wage structure for the Bank Wiring Observation Room was a complicated one, probably representing the interaction of past practices and new ideas in a subtle manner. (For a detailed account, see Roethlisberger and Dickson 1939: 409–12.) In essence, however, it amounted to a 'group piecework' scheme. The output levels of the individual workers were totalled, a piece rate was used to value this total, and the resulting fund was divided among the workers according to weights, termed 'hourly rates' in the study, that loosely reflected past productivity levels. That is, worker i received a wage of

$$W_i = \alpha_i w \bar{e} \tag{2.2}$$

where $\bar{e}$ is the average output of the n employees,[17] w is the piece rate, and α_i is a constant reflecting the hourly rate accorded to worker i, with $\alpha_i > 0$ for each i. Since we have represented the total wage fund in average terms, it follows that $\Sigma_i \alpha_i = n$.

---

[16] As a more general representation, let $U = U(W, e)$, where $U_W > 0$, $U_{WW} < 0$, $U_e < 0$, and $U_{ee} < 0$: the sign of U_{We} is unrestricted *a priori*. Then leisure – 'not supplying effort' – is a normal good if and only if

$$\frac{U_{WW} U_e}{U_W} > U_{We}.$$

Additive separability as in (2.1) implies that $U_{We} = 0$, so this inequality always holds, and the normality of leisure is guaranteed.

[17] For simplicity, I equate output and effort here. A more complicated production function would involve two types of interdependencies of the workers' actions. First, as here, effort levels might be interdependent through the piece rate, i.e. through the price. Second, and absent in the current model, effort levels might also be interdependent through an interdependence of marginal productivities, in physical terms. Obviously, any interdependency of this latter type can be represented through an interdependence via the piece rate – ultimately, workers care about the *value* of their output – so that this assumption is not at all restrictive.

The only element remaining in the specification of this model is the determination of the piece rate, w. We will find that the characteristics of the equilibrium depend critically upon the way in which the workers believe this rate is determined.

At the Hawthorne Plant, the Bank Wiring Observation Room rate was never changed during the seven months of the study; nor could the workers recall it ever being changed. Furthermore, 'changes in piece rates at the Western Electric Company . . . are not based upon the earnings of the worker. The company's policy is that piece rates will not be changed unless there is a change in the manufacturing process' (Roethlisberger and Dickson 1939: 534). Given these facts, the most natural assumption is to suppose that the workers believed the piece rate w to be constant:

$$w = k \qquad (2.3)$$

where k is an arbitrary positive constant.

In this case, with each worker maximizing (2.1), given (2.2) and (2.3), the non-cooperative Nash equilibrium effort level for agent i is defined implicitly by

$$\alpha_i \frac{k}{n} V'(\alpha_i k \bar{e}^*) = C_i'(e_i^*). \qquad (2.4)$$

At this equilibrium, if worker i would like worker j to raise his or her effort level − the first of the two sentiments quoted above − then, for $j \neq i$,

$$\frac{\partial U^{i*}}{\partial e_j^*} > 0, \qquad (2.5)$$

and conversely if i would like j to lower e_j^*, where U^{i*} denotes the utility of agent i at the optimum given by (2.4).[18] However, it is clear that, for all $j \neq i$,

$$\frac{\partial U^{i*}}{\partial e_j^*} = \alpha_i \frac{k}{n} V'(\alpha_i k \bar{e}^*) > 0 \qquad (2.6)$$

---

[18] Technically, a worker would put social pressure on another as long as the additional benefit of so doing exceeded its additional cost. Implicitly, I am omitting such costs from the model here for the sake of clarity, so that social pressure is applied according to the sign of the derivative in (2.5).

under the stated assumptions, so that this derivative can only be positive. The reason is obvious: the only effect of increasing e_j^* is to raise $\bar{e}^*$, so that, as agent i receives a constant share of the total wage fund, agent i always wants a higher level of e_j^*. Thus, if (2.3) holds, one cannot explain the two-sided pressure in this model.[19]

The natural change is to relax the assumption that the workers perceived the piece rate to be constant. There is some evidence, notwithstanding the company's declared policy and the actual constancy of the rate, that the workers may have held this view: see Roethlisberger and Dickson (1939: ch. XVIII). Of course, the reason why these apparent beliefs should have been maintained itself constitutes a puzzle, and we return to this at the end of this section.

Given that the piece rate may depend upon the output of the workers, an intuitive representation is that

$$w = f(\Sigma_i e_i) \tag{2.7}$$

where this revision schedule is presumed to be downward-sloping at all output levels. Then, proceeding as before, using (2.2) and (2.7) in (2.1), the equilibrium is characterized by

$$\alpha_i \left(f' \bar{e} + \frac{1}{n} f \right) V'(\cdot) = C_i'(\cdot) \tag{2.8}$$

where each of the derivatives in (2.8) is evaluated at the optimum. Then it follows that, for $j \neq i$,

---

[19] Note one other feature of this model which, in light of the Hawthorne evidence, is perhaps counter-intuitive. From (2.4), an implicit differentiation yields the result that

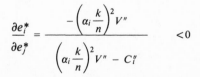

$$\frac{\partial e_i^*}{\partial e_j^*} = \frac{-\left(\alpha_i \dfrac{k}{n} \right)^2 V''}{\left(\alpha_i \dfrac{k}{n} \right)^2 V'' - C_i''} \qquad < 0$$

so that the model has negatively sloped reaction functions. The best response for j, if i works harder, is to ease off. While clearly consistent with the normality of leisure in the model − if i works harder, j's income rises holding e_i^* constant, so j supplies less effort − such a result seems implausible given the evidence from and the situation in the Hawthorne plant. The model to be developed in the next chapter, while allowing for such interdependencies of actions, also allows for social pressures producing positively sloped reaction functions.

$$\frac{\partial U^{i*}}{\partial e_j^*} = \alpha_i \left(f'\,\bar{e} + \frac{1}{n}f \right) V'(\cdot) \{ \gtreqless \} 0$$

$$<=> \quad \frac{f'\,\bar{e}}{f} \{ \gtreqless \} -\frac{1}{n}. \tag{2.9}$$

Thus, at the equilibrium, agent i would like agent j to increase his or her effort if the revision schedule is inelastic, and would like agent j to reduce his or her effort if the revision schedule is elastic. Again, the intuition is clear, with agent i's preference depending solely upon the change in the total wage fund, of which i receives a constant share.[20]

A consequence of (2.9) is that, given (2.7), the model cannot generate two-sided pressure. The reason is simple. At the equilibrium the revision schedule is either elastic or inelastic,[21] and hence, for *all* $j \neq i$, $\partial U^{i*}/\partial e_j^*$ is either negative or positive, respectively. Thus, it is possible for agent i to wish for an increase or a reduction in e_j^*, depending upon this elasticity. What is *not* possible, however, is that, for some agents j and k, agent i should want a higher value of e_j^* and a lower value of e_k^*. All workers' output levels enter (2.7) symmetrically, so only one-sided pressure can result.

An implication of this conclusion is that, if one wishes to generate two-sided pressure in this model, the output levels of the individual workers must enter the revision schedule in an asymmetric manner. Letting

$$w = f(e_1, \ldots, e_n) \tag{2.10}$$

with $f_i < 0$ for all i, and, using this in (2.1) and (2.2), it can be shown that

$$\frac{\partial U^{i*}}{\partial e_j^*} \{ \gtreqless \} 0 \quad <=> \quad \frac{f_j\,\bar{e}}{f} \{ \gtreqless \} -\frac{1}{n} \tag{2.11}$$

---

[20] There are two effects here. First, owing to the average effort reward schedule, an increase in e_j^* will raise agent i's wage, *ceteris paribus*. Second, an increase in e_j^* will imply a reduction of the piece rate, as determined by (2.7). The overall effect on i's wage of changing e_j^* depends on the relative magnitude of these two effects.

[21] It might have unitary elasticity, of course, in which case $\partial U^{i*}/\partial e_j^* = 0$.

where the parallel to (2.9) is clear. Hence, if there are two agents j and k in the group such that, when evaluated at the equilibrium,

$$f_j > \frac{-w}{n\bar{e}} > f_k.$$ (2.12)

then

$$\frac{\partial U^{i*}}{\partial e_j^*} > 0 \quad and \quad \frac{\partial U^{i*}}{\partial e_k^*} < 0.$$ (2.13)

The introduction of an asymmetry of the form (2.12) into the revision schedule can generate two-sided pressure.

A particular case of (2.10) is

$$w = \Sigma_i g(e_i)$$ (2.14)

where $g' < 0$, $g'' < 0$. Hence, the workers' output levels are evaluated in a similar manner, according to the same function $g(\cdot)$; but they do not enter the overall revision schedule symmetrically, owing to the curvature of $g(\cdot)$, provided that these output levels are heterogeneous.

Using (2.14), for $e_j < e_k$, we have that $g'(e_j) > g'(e_k)$, so that, if

$$g'(e_j) > \frac{-w}{n\bar{e}} > g'(e_k),$$ (2.15)

then it follows that

$$\frac{\partial U^{i*}}{\partial e_j^*} > 0 \quad and \quad \frac{\partial U^{i*}}{\partial e_k^*} < 0.$$ (2.16)

In this instance, agent i would like the low-output worker, agent j, to increase his or her output, and, simultaneously, would like the high-output worker, agent k, to reduce. Thus, (2.14) can generate the two-sided pressure found in the Hawthorne study.

Of course, this formulation begs the question of why a firm would adopt an asymmetric schedule such as (2.14). In the Hawthorne case, the question is, more precisely, why the workers would conjecture a schedule with this property, despite the constancy of the actual piece rate and despite the firm's declared policies. If the formulation of (2.1) and (2.2) is accurate, then it is unclear that assuming a conjectured asymmetry of the revision schedule − of exactly the right nature − is a sensible resolution of the Hawthorne puzzle.

There could be other strategic explanations, of course. One could assume that the firm is extracting information about potential productivity from the output of the most productive workers and basing the piece rate solely on these high-output levels, so that a worker would wish these workers to reduce their efforts while wanting the less productive to raise their output and hence raise $\bar{e}$. Or one could assume that workers have different conjectures, with the overall two-sided pressure resulting from the aggregation of these various preferences. And undoubtedly, other consistent rationales could be developed.[22]

None the less, in view of the failure of the natural, symmetric model, such an alternative explanation would of necessity have to be involved, and (to some degree) at odds with the Hawthorne evidence. In contrast, an explanation based upon conformity is straightforward, is consistent with the other evidence cited in this chapter, and, most important in this particular instance, is in tune with the Hawthorne researchers' own accounts. To cite just one of many similar remarks in *Management and the Worker*, 'The activities of the men in this group were directed inward toward maintaining their own social organization' (Roethlisberger and Dickson 1939: 535).

Finally, if we resolve the Hawthorne puzzle by the introduction of conformity, what do we make of the workers' statements about piece rate revisions? The simplest explanation is that of the researchers themselves, who were sceptical of all such declarations of motive. In discussing the apparent contradiction between the actual constancy of the piece rate and the expressed concerns of the workers, they wrote: 'None of the men had ever experienced any of the things they claimed they were guarding against; yet they acted as though they had' (Roethlisberger and Dickson 1939: 446). Later in the account, after a long discussion of all of this evidence, they concluded:

---

[22] Something could be made of letting the 'hourly rate', α_i, depend explicitly upon past output levels, of course. However, the complexity and, given the evidence, the implausibility of such a reading make it rather unattractive.

Their behavior was a way of affirming those sentiments which lay at the root of their group organization. [The reason given for their behaviour], far from being the 'cause' of their actions, was merely the way in which they rationalized their behavior. They attempted to give logical reasons for their conduct and to make it appear as though the latter was directed toward some outside interference, whereas in fact [the behaviour in restricting output] was primarily directed toward and expressed [the sentiments of the group]. [Roethlisberger and Dickson 1939: 534–5]

Implications

To the extent that agents conform to one another's behaviour patterns, two possible interpretations have been proposed, broadly speaking. According to the first of these, conformism is the product of processes of strategic interaction; a particular example of this is the case in which, as a means of information extraction, one agent uses other agents' actions as a guide to his or her own behaviour. In this way, fishing boats might cluster together in an apparently homogeneous sea, with the captains of the first boats out setting the location for the day. Or investors, seeing that others are buying a particular stock, might try to 'get in on a good thing', using the actions of others as a signal of underlying information.[23] In this view, then, the maxim, 'When in Rome, do as the Romans do', is solely a strategic one, based on informational factors.

The hallmark of this view, as the social psychology experiments pinpointed, is that, since there is no social interaction here, an agent's actions would be virtually unchanged if, instead of participating in a particular group, that agent merely observed the other group members' actions and then, having extracted the information, selected his or her own action. We say 'virtually' unchanged, of course, since an equilibrium in such a setting would be

---

[23] Henry Wallich has written about the most recent 'Radical Revision of the Distant Future' on the stock market — its behaviour since about 1973 — as follows: 'One might guess that [the reasons for this massive change in investment attitudes] have something to do with the professionalization of the securities business. Very likely this tends to homogenize views, increasing the herd instinct among bulls and bears, respectively ... There may be something to be learned from the history of mass delusions in the market after all' (Wallich 1979: 38). In this vein, see also Modigliani and Cohn (1979) and Ackley (1983). For an early classic discussion of these 'mass delusions', see Mackay (1852).

characterized by the agent reacting to the group members, each of whom in turn reacts to this agent's action, who in turn reacts to the group, and so on *ad infinitum*. To place the agent in isolation would curtail this process after one step.

Two things seem clear about this interpretation of conformity. First, there is essentially nothing in this view that does not fit very naturally into a conventional economic model. A theme in the economic literature over the past 20 years, at least, has been that information may be revealed by actions. Thus, to cite just three prominent examples, a prospective buyer of a used car may regard the owner's willingness to sell as an indication that it may be a 'lemon' (Akerlof 1970); a potential employer may regard educational achievements as a signal of underlying ability (Spence 1974); and prices themselves, the result of agents' actions in markets, may reveal otherwise private information in a rational expectations equilibrium (e.g. Radner 1979). Hence, aside from the particularities of the situation in question, the informational reading of conformity poses no real problems for economic theory.

The second point about this strategic view, as was manifest in our earlier discussion, is that it is insufficient to explain all aspects of conformity. The unimportance that it ascribes to social interaction, which I have noted as the distinctive feature of this paradigm, is evidently a weakness in many instances, with the Hawthorne puzzle being a clear but by no means remarkable example.

Accordingly, it seems appropriate seriously to consider the alternative view of conformism proposed above. This reading – that conformity arises as a consequence of a desire to be accepted by a group – is in sharp contrast to the informational perspective. First, the role of social interaction now becomes a critical one: agents take actions mindful of what the other group members will think of them as a result. The interactional processes, which might range from a subtle tone of voice to an overt act of social ostracism, are the key. Hence, in this light, 'When in Rome, do as the Romans do' is socially based advice, taking into account both an intrinsic self-motivation to conform and the potential reactions of the Romans, should one not conform.

Second, the socially based interpretation of conformity, unlike the alternative approach, poses an unfamiliar problem for economic theory. In this view, agents select actions not just by making the usual marginal trade-off between the utility of wage income and the disutility of effort, as they would were they making these choices in isolation. In addition, they are aware of the costs of selecting an action unike that selected by the other group members − the social costs of nonconformity − and, in maximizing their utility, they are also aware of trade-offs between their other objectives and these socially based costs of nonconformity. It is this type of theory that will be developed and analysed in the chapters to come.

3

A Model of Conformist Behaviour

In this chapter I shall begin to develop an economic theory of social influence by constructing a model of conformism. My strategy is to characterize behaviour as depending upon two types of factors: the individualistic, or 'private', elements of opportunities and preferences, as typically comprise an economic theory; and the social aspects of behaviour in group situations, usually termed 'social influence' by the social psychologist. By so doing, a theory can be developed in which tastes, opportunities, and the social environment together combine to determine an agent's action.

The context of the model, as mentioned above, is the workplace, and the theory will concern the behaviour of members of a working group. One might draw an analogy between this particular model and, say, the workers in the Hawthorne study whose behaviour was examined in chapter 2. However, it is probably not terribly useful to press this parallel too far since, like any actual workplace, the Hawthorne plant had many singular features which must be abstracted from in developing a theoretical model.

The reasons for selecting this example are twofold. First, it is clear that customary and normative behaviour is of prime importance in the workplace and in the labour market, and some of our earlier discussion alluded to the potential economic significance that this might have. Many writers have stressed the fact that, typically, while the time a worker spends at the workplace can be monitored, it is more difficult to monitor a worker's effort. This has long been a central contention in Marxist economics, where a distinction is drawn between 'labour power', which is hired by a firm, and 'labour', which is the input actually used in production. Some recent work in this area has yielded both microeconomic consequences (e.g. Edwards 1979) and macroeconomic implications (e.g. Bowles 1983, Bowles, Gordon, and Weisskopf 1983).

Many non-Marxist economists have also focused on this distinction, arguing that the incentive for imperfectly monitored workers to supply suboptimal levels of effort — a moral hazard problem — mandates the existence of a residual claimant who can perform supervision so as to minimize such shirking (e.g. Alchian and Demsetz 1972, Holmström 1982). Finally, and perhaps most important, several writers have noted potential macroeconomic consequences of the fact that workers can choose how hard to work (e.g. Schlicht 1978, Solow 1979b, Akerlof 1982, Stoft 1982, Shapiro and Stiglitz 1982, Eaton and White 1983), using this aspect of behaviour within a firm to generate a type of 'efficiency wage' theory of involuntary unemployment.

Thus, the tradition of examining workers' decisions about effort is a venerable one. Moreover, although few of these models have addressed the issue, Akerlof's (1982) paper being an exception, I argued above that, in such a context, it natural to think that there may be a type of social interdependence in these levels of effort chosen by the workers. The model developed below can be seen as precisely an illustration of such an interdependence.[1]

Second, as was briefly mentioned in the opening chapter, the example is useful because of the clarity such specificity lends to the analysis. That is, the example — any example — facilitates a straightforward exposition, whereas a general treatment might be overly abstract, even abstruse. As was stressed at the outset, the idea underlying the theory goes beyond the particular case of workplace behaviour, and the breadth of the evidence in the previous chapter indicated this potential generality. In subsequent chapters some of the broader issues raised by the theory will be considered.

Before proceeding, one important point should be made. It is of

---

[1] Ishikawa (1981) developed an innovative model incorporating an 'emulation effect', based upon both 'pride' and 'shame', thereby criticizing the 'shirking—monitoring' view of the capitalist firm organization dominant in earlier work. His paper bears a family resemblance to the model of this chapter, although it is clear that, from both a social—psychological and an economic perspective, there are critical differences between conformism and an analysis based upon pride and shame. I would like to thank Professor Ishikawa for making an English translation of his paper available to me.

at, in many actual situations, both strategic and social onformism may be present. For the present treatment, focus on those social and normative aspects of t produce a conformity of actions, although later in .... shall consider how such socially based conformism can interact with a variety of strategic aspects of economic behaviour. The reason for restricting the modelling to these social rationales for conformism is simply that, as noted in chapter 2, this aspect of social influence is novel to the economist, whereas an informational reading is not.

The Basic Model

The model that I shall develop concerns the actions of workers who are employed by one firm and who work in a group context. I shall seek to address how, in addition to being concerned about those variables upon which economists usually focus — the wage and the disutility of effort — these workers might interact in a social sense, producing some conformism in their decisions in the workplace. In constructing such a theory, there is often a trade-off between generality and clarity, and my choice is to make the underlying concept transparent in as simple a way as possible. Accordingly, I shall make a number of particular assumptions for expositional purposes. Most of the aspects of the model can be readily generalized, and below I shall note explicitly where an assumption is, in a sense to be made clear, critical to the structure of the theory.

Behaviour of Firms

A large number of firms is envisaged, each of which produces homogeneous output, q, which it is able to sell without limit at a constant price, p, the market for final goods being perfectly competitive. Output is produced using labour, measured in units of effort, and each employee of a firm faces a production function of the form:

$$q_i = f_i(e_i) \qquad (3.1)$$

where q_i is the output of the ith worker, e_i is his or her effort, and each f_i is increasing and concave in e_i: additional effort generates more output, but at a declining rate. Total output at a firm is then given by summing all the individual output levels, so if a firm employs n workers, this total is just[2]

$$\sum_{i=1}^{n} q_i.$$

Each firm faces two types of costs. First, for each employee hired it must pay a given fixed cost, T. This cost represents managerial expenses and the cost of hiring and training, and it is fixed in the sense that it is independent of the level of output that the employee produces.[3] Second, each firm pays each of its workers a wage that depends on the output that the worker produces, so that worker i producing output q_i receives a wage of $W(q_i)$. Hence the total variable cost − the cost that depends immediately upon the level of output − is given by

$$\sum_{i=1}^{n} W(q_i).$$

Overall, then, if firm j hires n workers, it has profits given by

$$\Pi_j = p\sum_{i=1}^{n} q_i - \sum_{i=1}^{n} W(q_i) - nT. \qquad (3.2)$$

I shall often restrict my attention to the case of pure piece rate wages, so that $W(q_i) = wq_i$, where w is the piece rate.

---

[2] A critical assumption of this theory is that, in fact, workers have to work in groups; otherwise no social interactions would arise. One could guarantee that this is indeed the case as an endogenous outcome by, for example, introducing some increasing returns at this point, thereby ensuring that one-worker firms are forced out of business by the more profitable multi-worker units. It is clearer, however, to keep to the simple additive production function given in the text, taking the phenomenon of group output as an innocuous working assumption.

[3] Increasing returns arising from the spreading of overhead and managerial costs could be associated with this cost declining as more workers are hired at a given firm. Since constant returns are assumed elsewhere, however, it is both clearer and more consistent to maintain that assumption here as well, so that T is the same for every employee hired.

Behaviour of Workers

It is assumed that workers are heterogeneous in both abilities and tastes. This former diversity is represented by the fact that different workers have different production functions, as indicated by the subscript i of $f_i(\cdot)$ in (3.1). The heterogeneity in tastes is captured by assuming that workers are idiosyncratic with regard to the disutility of effort, as will be specified in a moment.

The ith worker is seen as maximizing a utility function of the following form:

$$U^i = U^i[\, W(q_i), e_i, d(q_i, q_{-i})\,].\tag{3.3}$$

Worker i maximizes (3.3) by choosing e_i, his or her effort supply, and we make the standard Nash type of assumption that he or she selects this e_i taking the actions of the other workers as given.[4] In (3.3), the first argument of the utility function is worker i's wage, and, as is standard, we presume that, for each i, $U^i_1 > 0$ and $U^i_{11} \leqslant 0$, where a subscript k indicates a partial derivative with respect to the kth argument of the function. Hence, utility is increasing in the wage, but at a declining rate. The second argument of (3.3) is worker i's effort, and, in conformity with usual practice, it is assumed that, for each i, $U^i_2 < 0$, $U^i_{22} \leqslant 0$, so utility is decreasing and concave in effort. The heterogeneity across workers with respect to this disutility of effort is indicated by the superscript i on U^i in (3.3). Finally, the third argument of the utility function is a measure of the distance between worker i's output level, q_i, and the output levels of the other members of the working group, q_{-i}. It is assumed that $U^i_3 < 0$, $U^i_{33} \leqslant 0$, while no restrictions, aside from symmetry, are placed on the signs of the cross-partials.

It is the third term of (3.3), of course, that represents the novelty inherent in this model. According to this specification, workers dislike supplying a level of effort that is, judged by the metric $d(\cdot, \cdot)$, far from the output levels of the other members of the working group. This desire for some conformism, arising from the types of group considerations and social influence discussed in the

---

[4] For an interesting discussion of an alternative, in a different economic context, see Bresnahan (1981).

previous chapter, is the key to this model.[5] I have chosen to represent this as a function of relative output levels, rather than in terms
of the effort levels supplied, since this is consistent with output being
public knowledge, while the effort that worker i supplies remains
his or her private knowledge.[6]

Finally, it is assumed that each worker supplies his or her labour
to a firm provided that the utility from so doing exceeds his or her
exogenously given reservation utility level, $\bar{U}^i$. Reflecting the differences in abilities in the population of workers, there will be a
distribution of these reservation utility levels. However, for
simplicity it will be assumed that, for all agents, the reservation utility
constraint never binds in equilibrium.

Characteristics of the Labour Market

Two particular assumptions are made about the functioning of the
labour market which permit a simple analysis. First, it is assumed
that, from the population of heterogeneous agents, a firm hires the
members of its working group without knowledge of their
characteristics. Of course, one could weaken this assumption by
allowing a situation in which, at some cost, the firm is able to infer

---

[5] A somewhat subtle question arises regarding the social psychological interpretation of the
evidence cited in chapter 2: did it indicate an active desire to conform, or, alternatively, did it
show conformism resulting from agents desiring to be emulated? The significance of this
distinction is that it may impinge upon the interpretation of the manner in which I have
modelled conformism. If the former reading of the evidence is valid, then the specification in
(3.3) seems exactly correct. If, on the other hand, the latter interpretation holds, then one
can regard (3.3) as a type of reduced-form characterization, representing a complex set of
implicit and explicit social sanctions and the workers' various responses to these potential
pressures. Durkheim seems to have favoured the second of these interpretations: 'If I do not
submit to the conventions of society, if in my dress I do not conform to the customs observed
in my country and in my class, the ridicule I provoke, the social isolation in which I am kept,
produce, although in an attenuated form, the same effects as a punishment in the strict sense
of the word' (1938: 2–3). However, the evidence in chapter 2 can also be used to buttress the
former reading. Overall, it seems that both views have some merit. In either case, of course,
the conformism arises for social reasons, and as such it remains a novelty in an economic
analysis.

[6] Alternative assumptions – such as caring about both the conformity in effort levels and
the conformity in output, to varying degrees – produce only minor changes in the results to
follow.

such information, perhaps imperfectly.[7] For clarity, however, I make the 'extreme ignorance' assumption here.[8]

Second, it is assumed that both the firm and the workers are aware that, once they are contractually linked, there are considerable costs associated with a severance of these ties. These costs, which are not specified in detail here, might result from, for example, training expenses, the development of specific human capital, legal expenses, and possible declines in morale resulting from high labour turnover.[9] Their effect is to make it prohibitively expensive either for a worker to move from firm to firm or for a firm to hire and fire repeatedly.[10]

It should be noted, at this point, that in a sense these assumptions are critical. For conformism to have any bite, there must be some heterogeneity in the group of workers: otherwise, in a symmetric equilibrium, perfect conformity follows trivially. Thus, there must be (at most) an imperfect sorting of worker types, leaving some residual differences among the workers. The two assumptions just given, which present an extreme benchmark case of no sorting at all, either before or after the worker is hired, provide a limiting case, though the essence of the results clearly carries over to any situation in which a completely perfect sorting is not achieved. Needless to say, this is probably the case in every real-world firm and working group.

Equilibrium

In equilibrium, the typical worker *i* supplies an effort level of e_i to maximize (3.3) subject to the condition that the utility from so doing

---

[7] Related work, which studies the process of a firm accumulating information specific to workers, has been conducted by, among others, MacDonald (1980) and Burdett and Mortensen (1981).

[8] Notwithstanding the references in the preceding note, there may be something to commend this 'extreme ignorance' assumption. In a detailed case-study of the hiring practices of a large conglomerate in the San Francisco Bay Area, Swartz concluded that, 'in spite of the company's use of complex information in the hiring process, no evidence was found that the people hired are *ex ante* more likely to do well than those not hired' (1981: 93).

[9] Parsons (1972) is a classic reference that documents the empirical importance of specific human capital. See also the 'toll model' developed in Okun (1981).

[10] Implicitly, I assume that these costs would be divided so that both sides would bear part of the total cost associated with separation, perhaps as the solution to a Nash bargaining problem.

exceeds his or her reservation utility, $\bar{U}^i$. In making this choice of an optimal e_i, the worker trades off among three variables: the desire for wage income, the distaste of effort, and the disutility resulting from supplying an output level far from those of the other group members. As noted before, it is this third consideration that is the key to the model. Given this behaviour, the typical firm j, having randomly picked n such workers from the population, has an average output level of $\bar{q}^j$. Reflecting the distribution of tastes and abilities in the population of workers, there is a distribution $G(\bar{q})$ of average output levels across firms. In the pure piece rate case, this implies that the equilibrium piece rate $w*$ is determined endogenously, given p and T, as

$$w* = p - \frac{T}{\int \bar{q} dG(\bar{q})} \tag{3.4}$$

where $\int \bar{q} dG(\bar{q})$ is the average output taken across all of the firms in the economy. Hence, at this equilibrium, firm j has profits given by

$$\Pi_j = nT \left[\frac{\bar{q}_j}{\int \bar{q} dG(\bar{q})} - 1 \right] \tag{3.5}$$

and, by the construction of $w*$, a potential entrant expects to make zero profits. Of those in business in this short-run equilibrium, the lucky firms earn positive profits, while the unlucky, though losing money, are still able to cover their variable costs.

The interest of this equilibrium, of course, lies in precisely how the third term of (3.3) alters the actions that the workers select. This could be characterized in quite general terms, but it seems clearer instead to focus on a more particular instance of conformism, keeping this present general concept of equilibrium in the background.

A Specific Parameterization

In this section, some particular assumptions are adopted as to the form of (3.1) and (3.3). This will enable a clear analysis of the nature of the equilibrium, so that the social interdependence of workers' actions can be examined. Of course, while such particularity is valuable in rendering the model tractable, it does imply that the results are, strictly speaking, equally particular. However, although the quantitative conclusions are necessarily affected by these assumptions, the qualitative results need not be so affected, and, indeed, most of the implications to follow do not seem to be artefacts of this specific parameterization.

The Nash Equilibrium

Suppose that all workers are of identical ability, and that effort is measured in such a way that, for each i,

$$q_i = e_i. \tag{3.6}$$

Further, suppose that each worker maximizes a modified quadratic utility function:

$$U^i = W(e_i) - b_i e_i^2 - c \sum_{j=1}^{n} (e_i - e_j)^2 \tag{3.7}$$

where, as a result of the trivial production function (3.6), q_i has been replaced by e_i throughout. The first term reflects worker i's wage income: initially it will be assumed that $W(e_i) = we_i$, the pure piece rate case. The second term represents the agent's disutility of effort, with $b_i > 0$ for all i and $b_i \neq b_j$ in general: thus, agents differ in their disutility of effort. The final term, which is assumed identical for all agents,[11] represents the conformity element, the consequences of which will be derived: it is assumed that $c \geqslant 0$, thereby nesting a more standard model as the special case when $c = 0$.

Finally, for ease of exposition, suppose initially that $n = 2$, so each worker is in a group with one other. I shall show below that nothing of importance hinges upon this assumption.

Proceeding in a straightforward way under a Nash assumption, so that i believes that $\partial e_j / \partial e_i = 0$, the necessary conditions for the maximization of (3.7) imply that

---

[11] The introduction of differing conformity parameters is elementary, and its consequences are omitted.

$$e_1 = \frac{w + 2ce_2}{2(b_1 + c)} \tag{3.8}$$

where, as throughout, the symmetric expression for e_2 is omitted. Figure 3.1 illustrates this reaction function, together with that of worker 2. These reaction functions have non-negative slopes in general, and a positive slope for $c > 0$, which is the case assumed in figure 3.1. This reflects the conformism characteristic of the model.

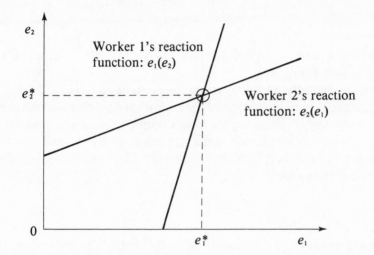

FIGURE 3.1 The Nash equilibrium. The circle denotes an equilibrium point.

Using (3.8), at the Nash equilibrium (e_1^*, e_2^*) in figure 3.1,

$$e_1 = \frac{(b_2 + 2c)w}{2[b_1 b_2 + (b_1 + b_2)c]} \tag{3.9}$$

where, for notational simplicity, the asterisks denoting an optimal choice of e_1 are omitted. The linear first-order conditions give a unique equilibrium, and it is non-degenerate whenever $w > 0$, $c > 0$, and $b_i > 0$ for both i.[12]

---

[12] The two reaction functions have positive intercepts equal to $w/2(b_i + c)$, $i = 1,2$. Additionally, worker 1's reaction function has a slope of $(b_1 + c)/c > 1$, while worker 2's has a slope of $c/(b_2 + c) < 1$, under the stated assumptions, so that the non-degeneracy of the equilibrium is guaranteed.

Hence, given a draw (b_1, b_2) from the population of workers, firm j has profits equal to

$$\Pi_j = (p - w^*)(e_1 + e_2) - 2T \qquad (3.10)$$

where the e_i are found from (3.9), and, averaging across all such firms, a piece rate equal to

$$w^* = p - \frac{T}{\int \bar{e}dG(\bar{e})} \qquad (3.11)$$

results in a competitive equilibrium where a potential entrant makes zero expected profits.

More generally, (3.9) illustrates the contention made in the introduction to this chapter; that is, the actions of a worker depend upon his or her tastes, b_1 and c, his or her opportunities, w^*, and his or her 'social environment', here summarized by b_2 and c. This dependence can best be seen by consideration of the comparative statics of the model.

Comparative Statics

Some properties of the model can be highlighted by comparing the two Nash equilibria that result when only one element producing the final outcome differs between these equilibria. I shall illustrate some of these results graphically, although when it is clearer just to calculate the comparative statics, I shall do so analytically.

First, the model has standard properties with respect to differing opportunities or preferences. If we consider two equilibria, α and β, where the piece rates differ, say $w^\alpha > w^\beta$, then it is clear that more effort is supplied when the higher piece rate w^α prevails (figure 3.2): both reaction functions shift out in a parallel manner. Also, if we consider two equilibria where only worker 1's disutility of effort parameter differs between them, with, say, $b_1^\alpha > b_1^\beta$, then a similar graph (figure 3.3) illustrates how less effort is supplied when the disutility of effort is higher (case α): worker 1's reaction function shifts to the left and becomes steeper.

Second, the effort that worker 1 supplies depends, at the equilibrium, upon the 'social environment' in which the worker is placed,

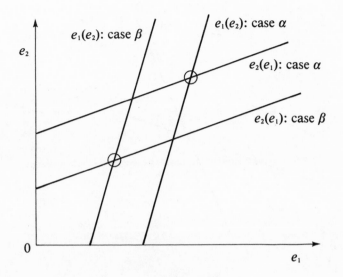

FIGURE 3.2　The effect of a difference in the piece rate: $w^\alpha > w^\beta$. The circles denote equilibrium points.

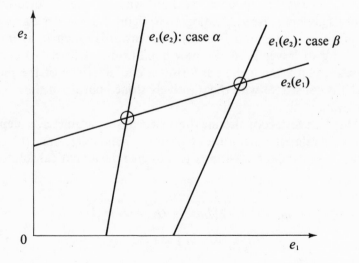

FIGURE 3.3　The effect of a difference in worker 1's disutility of effort: $b_1^\alpha > b_1^\beta$. The circles denote equilibrium points.

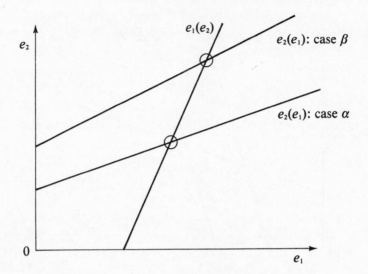

FIGURE 3.4   The effect of a difference in worker 2's disutility of effort: $b_2^\alpha > b_2^\beta$. The circles denote equilibrium points.

represented, in the context of this model, by b_2 and c. If we hold c constant, then in the usual way, for $b_2^\alpha > b_2^\beta$, it follows (figure 3.4) that less effort is supplied by worker 1 when worker 2's disutility of effort is greater (case α). Analogous to figure 3.3, worker 2's reaction function is flatter and is shifted downwards when b_2 is higher, resulting in lower e_1 at the new equilibrium. Clearly, this result comes directly from the conformism characteristic of the model, and it is consistent with the positively sloped nature of the reaction functions.

Third, the effect of altering the conformism parameter, c, depends upon the relative magnitudes of e_1 and e_2, and here, since the graph is rather intricate, it is simpler just to give the analytical solution:

$$\frac{\partial e_1}{\partial c} = \frac{b_2(b_1 - b_2)w}{2[b_1 b_2 + (b_1 + b_2)c]^2}$$

$$\{\gtreqless\} \ 0 \quad \text{as} \quad b_1 \ \{\gtreqless\} \ b_2. \tag{3.12}$$

If $b_1 > b_2$, then the effort that worker 1 supplies will be no greater than that supplied by worker 2, and since an increased degree of conformism will reduce the distance between these effort levels, it will raise e_1 and lower e_2, and conversely when $b_2 > b_1$.

Observed Conformity

In addition to the present characterization of conformism as the slope of an agent's reaction function, it may also be of interest to examine a measure of the distance between e_1 and e_2, since, in the original motivation, it was this that the conformist sought to reduce through an appropriate choice of effort level. Indeed, although the present results are interesting *per se*, it would perhaps not be a wholly satisfying treatment of conformity unless it related, in the way that seems intuitive, to measures of the distance between the e_i. After all, it is presumably this distance that is actually observed.

As with the result of (3.12), it is possible to illustrate conclusions about 'observed conformity' graphically, but it is probably easiest simply to calculate the comparative statics. Adopting this strategy, and letting $|e_1 - e_2|$ be a measure of the distance between e_1 and e_2,

$$\frac{\partial |e_1 - e_2|}{\partial w} = \frac{|b_2 - b_1| w}{2[b_1 b_2 + (b_1 + b_2)c]} \geq 0. \qquad (3.13)$$

The wage expansion path, in (e_1, e_2) space, is a ray from the origin, so that, except when $e_1 = e_2$, a higher wage rate increases the distance between the e_i in equilibrium. Equivalently, were we to employ a distance measure that adjusted appropriately for magnitudes of e_1 and e_2, it would follow that this would be invariant with respect to changes in the piece rate.

There is also the result that

$$\frac{\partial |e_1 - e_2|}{\partial b_1} = \text{sign}(b_1 - b_2) \frac{b_2(b_2 + 2c)w}{2[b_1 b_2 + (b_1 + b_2)c]^2}$$

$$\{ \gtrless \} 0 \text{ as } b_1 \{ \gtrless \} b_2. \qquad (3.14)$$

If $b_1 < b_2$, so that $e_1 > e_2$ for all finite levels of c, then an increase in worker 1's disutility of effort parameter will, in equilibrium, imply a lower supply of effort by worker 1: and similarly for $b_1 > b_2$.

Moreover, the change in e_1 following a change in b_1 exceeds the associated change in e_2, thereby yielding the result (3.14).

Finally, a simple calculation shows that

$$\frac{\partial \, | \, e_1 - e_2 \, |}{\partial c} = \frac{-(b_1 + b_2) \, | \, b_2 - b_1 \, | \, w}{2 [b_1 b_2 + (b_1 + b_2)c]^2} \leqslant 0. \qquad (3.15)$$

A higher value of the conformity parameter c is associated, in equilibrium, with a larger degree of static, observed conformism, so that $| \, e_1 - e_2 \, |$ is lower. This shows that the two concepts are related as one would intuitively wish.

A Resolution of The Hawthorne Puzzle

Finally, before examining some extensions of this model, note how the present structure yields a straightforward resolution of the Hawthorne puzzle posed in chapter 2. The objective is to demonstrate the presence of 'two-sided pressure' (see p. 28 above), and to do this I shall maintain the parameterization of (3.6) and (3.7) but will let $n = 3$, this being the minimum group size that permits such two-sided pressure.

Directly from (3.7), it can be seen that, at the non-cooperative equilibrium, for $j = 2, 3$, then

$$\frac{\partial U^{1*}}{\partial e_j^*} = 2c(e_1^* - e_j^*). \qquad (3.16)$$

Thus, exactly as in the Hawthorne study, if $e_3^* < e_1^* < e_2^*$ in equilibrium, then

$$\frac{\partial U^{1*}}{\partial e_3^*} > 0 \quad and \quad \frac{\partial U^{1*}}{\partial e_2^*} < 0. \qquad (3.17)$$

That is, agent 1 would like to put pressure both on the slower worker (agent 3) to speed up, and on the faster worker (agent 2) to slow down, which corresponds precisely to the Hawthorne evidence from the Bank Wiring Observation Room.

Some Extensions

In this section, a number of possible extensions are considered to the simple model developed above. Some of these avenues are relatively straightforward additions to the above theory, indicating that, while particular, there was nothing terribly pathological in the assumptions made in that treatment. Other extensions are more substantial, however, and can be seen as suggesting an area for future work.

As previously noted, many economists have addressed aspects of behaviour in groups, focusing particularly upon problems of moral hazard associated with public good phenomena in such a setting. An example would be a situation in which, receiving some share of the value of the total output of the group in wages, a worker may have an incentive to slack off, free-riding upon the output levels of the others (see, e.g., Miyazaki 1984). One might term this type of circumstance as one of 'indirect interdependence', in that worker i cares about his or her fellow workers' output levels indirectly, through the effect they have on the wage that worker i receives. In contrast, the social influence characteristic of the present model could be termed 'direct interdependence', as one worker cares about the others' actions *per se*. Much past work has been done on the nature and consequences of various types of indirect interdependence, and a fascinating area deserving more study is how, when combined, direct interdependence of a social nature and indirect, strategic interdependencies can interact. I give a few examples of the possible outcomes below, but clearly many other cases remain to be examined.

Two-part Wage Structures

Rather than pay a pure piece rate of the type analysed above, firms may offer a partial piece rate wage structure of the form:

$$W_i = \beta + \alpha e_i. \tag{3.18}$$

These time rate−piece rate schemes, once termed 'Manchester guarantees', are empirically common (see, e.g., Belcher 1974 and Patten 1967), and they may be adopted for a variety of reasons. For example, risk aversion on the part of workers could play a role if random factors affect e_i (Stiglitz 1975), with the wage schedule trading off stability of income against a loss of incentives. Envy among the group could also induce a desire for greater homogeneity of wage levels. Finally, the firm itself may introduce a two-part structure, seeking to generate self-selection among the workers.

Whatever the reason, the introduction of (3.18) produces an indirect interdependency in equilibrium among the workers' actions. At that competitive equilibrium, taking the price of output as unity,

$$\Sigma_i W_i = \Sigma_i e_i \tag{3.19}$$

and hence

$$W_i = (1 - \alpha)\bar{e} + \alpha e_i \tag{3.20}$$

so that the wage that agent i receives is a weighted average of the average output of the group, $\bar{e}$, and the output that i produces, e_i, with this weight being the slope of the payment schedule.[13] The workers' actions are indirectly interdependent since, except when $\alpha = 1$, e_j affects $\bar{e}$ and hence W_i.[14]

Using (3.20) in an appropriately modified version of (3.7) – so that worker i's wage can depend on both e_i and $\bar{e}$ – the Nash equilibrium level of effort is given by

$$e_1 = \frac{(1 + \alpha)(b_2 + 2c)}{4[b_1 b_2 + (b_1 + b_2)c]}. \tag{3.21}$$

In this instance, effort is an increasing function of α, the slope of the payment schedule. Thus, an average output wage ($\alpha = 0$) produces lower effort levels than a pure piece rate ($\alpha = 1$). In turn, the pure piece rate is associated with lower levels of effort than an 'entrance fee' wage schedule ($\alpha > 1$), where workers pay a fee to

---

[13] Rewriting (3.18) as $W_i = \bar{e} + \alpha(e_i - \bar{e})$, one can also interpret the two-part wage structure as the payment of an average output wage, combined with an incentive scheme rewarding output in excess of the average and penalizing that below it.

[14] Note that, in this case, the indirect interactions associated with this wage schedule can give rise to negatively sloped reaction functions for appropriate parameter values. As mentioned, Miyazaki (1984) contains an illuminating analysis of this case. Compare also note 19 to chapter 2 above.

earn the right to a highly sloped wage schedule. Of course, the implication that, as α is further increased, e_i also increases without limit is an unrealistic one, and should be seen rather as an artefact of the quadratic specification. In a more general setting, one would eventually expect income effects to swamp the substitution effect, so that after some point, effort supply would not continue to increase even if the piece rate were raised still further.

Piece Rate Revisions

Another interesting extension, especially in light of the 'Hawthorne puzzle' and similar evidence, is to examine how the presence of a desire for conformity alters workers' strategic responses to a piece rate revision schedule. The basic idea is simple. The presence of conformity acts to alter the incentive structure, and, as is intuitive, to generate a tendency towards a 'cooperative' type of solution.

I use the quadratic parameterization with the group size fixed at 2 to illustrate this result. Each worker maximizes a utility function of the form:

$$U^i = w(e_1, e_2)e_i - b_ie_i^2 - c(e_i - e_j)^2 \qquad (3.22)$$

where the only novelty relative to (3.7) is the first term, showing the explicit dependence of the piece rate upon the output of the workers. Clearly, this is a model of a non-competitive firm — otherwise the piece rate would be taken as given, as earlier — and it is convenient to assume that it sets the piece rate as a linear function of output levels: this will then yield linear reaction functions, and thereby enable an easy calculation of the equilibrium. Hence, it is assumed that

$$w(e_1, e_2) = g - h(e_1 + e_2) \qquad (3.23)$$

where constants g and h are both positive. This revision schedule is taken to be common knowledge.

Given (3.23), the reaction functions have the form

$$e_1 = \frac{g + (2c - h)e_2}{2(b_1 + c + h)} \qquad (3.24)$$

which has a positive slope if and only if $c > h/2$. The economic reason for this is straightforward. If c is zero, so there is no desire for conformity, then the only reason worker 1 cares about e_2 is because of (3.23), and, to the extent that e_2 is small (large), the marginal return through wages for a unit of effort supplied by worker 1 is large (small). Hence, without conformity, the reaction functions would be 'nonconformist', having a negative slope. The introduction of conformity offsets this effect, and if c is large enough the reaction functions will have a positive slope in spite of (3.23).

The desired result now follows directly from (3.24). Solving for the non-cooperative Nash equilibrium levels of effort, and summing them to yield the total, $E = e_1 + e_2$, a little algebra reveals that

$$\frac{\partial^2 E}{\partial h\, \partial c} \geqslant 0 \qquad (3.25)$$

where the inequality is strict except when $b_1 = b_2$, the case of identical workers. That is, the response to a piece rate revision schedule, $\partial E / \partial h$, is always negative; and (3.25) establishes that this response is increasing in the degree of conformity.

A discrete example conveys the intuition that underlies (3.25). For $c < h/2$, the reaction functions have negative slope. In this case, if, for whatever reason, worker 1 restricts output, then the best response of worker 2 is to increase e_2: but clearly, this reaction by worker 2 undermines worker 1's output restriction, since the revision schedule is based on the sum of their outputs. Conversely, for $c > h/2$, the reaction functions have a positive slope, and, should worker 1 restrict output, the best response for worker 2 is to follow suit: in contrast to the nonconformist case, this conformist behaviour reinforces the effect of worker 1's output restriction on the piece rate. Hence, to generalize this example, once it is recognized that the payoff to individual output restriction depends upon the degree of conformity, the result of (3.25) follows directly: the response to a piece rate revision is greater, the greater is the degree of conformism.

Finally, we note that this result illustrates something of a relationship between cooperation and conformity. To the extent that conformity is present, and agents correctly take it into account in making their private, non-cooperative decisions, the outcome can often resemble a type of cooperative outcome. Here, as the degree of conformity increases, the workers restrict output to a greater degree for any given revision schedule, moving towards the collectively rational situation in which, like imperfect competitors, they exploit (3.23) by curtailing production. This relationship will be pursued further in the next extension.

An Alternative Solution Concept

The equilibrium levels of effort derived above in the basic model were inefficient. This inefficiency arose since, in the non-cooperative maximization of his or her own utility, agent i ignored the effect of his or her choice of e_i upon the utility of the other worker in the group, U^j. In particular, the utility possibility frontier − the set of (e_1, e_2) pairs that maximize $\lambda_1 U^1 + \lambda_2 U^2$ as the weights λ_1 and λ_2 vary − would have been characterized by a lower level of total effort, taking into account the externality produced by the desire for conformity.

Accordingly, it might be sensible to examine a cooperative type of solution to this model. Maximizing $U^1 + U^2$ by choice of e_1 and e_2, and maintaining the Nash assumption, this solution is

$$e_1^C = \frac{(b_2 + 4c)w}{2[b_1b_2 + (b_1 + b_2)2c]}. \qquad (3.26)$$

Comparing this with the non-cooperative solution (3.9), the only difference is that, as one would expect, the conformity parameter c here receives twice as much weight. As a result, denoting the earlier non-cooperative solution by e_1^N, then

$$e_1^N > e_1^C \iff b_1 < b_2. \qquad (3.27)$$

If $b_1 < b_2$, so that e_1 exceeds e_2 − a result that holds under either solution concept for finite values of c − then a greater pressure towards conformity, as in the cooperative type of solution, will lead to a smaller level of effort, compared with the less conformist, non-cooperative case.

Overall, however, these effects do not cancel out, except in the degenerate case of identical agents. Letting $E^k = \Sigma_i e_i^k$, where

$k = N, C$ and denotes the solution concept employed, the result follows that

$$E^N > E^C \iff (b_1 - b_2)^2 c \geqslant 0. \qquad (3.28)$$

Thus, compared with the non-cooperative solution, this 'cooperative' equilibrium is characterized by lower aggregate effort supply. The intuition behind this result, which mirrors the reasons underlying the inefficiency of the non-cooperative outcome, is that since the utility loss from nonconformity depends upon the magnitude of $(e_1 - e_2)^2$, there is a tendency to reduce e_i, at the margin, so as to reduce this collective utility loss.

Another aspect of (3.28) arises as the degree of conformity becomes large. Intuitively, it might be expected that, as the agents become increasingly concerned to choose 'close' actions, the difference between the non-cooperative Nash equilibrium and the cooperative type of solution would become small. Such a result, which provides something of a foundation for linking cooperation and conformity, does indeed obtain, subject to two caveats. The first of these is that, since the cooperative solution itself is a function of c, one cannot speak of the non-cooperative solution approaching 'the' cooperative outcome as the degree of conformity increases. Rather, both solutions alter as c alters, but their difference becomes small as c grows large. The second caveat is that, if c becomes infinite, the reaction functions in both the cooperative and the non-cooperative case coincide with the 45° line in (e_1, e_2) space, and indeterminacy ensues: if all that matters is conformity, then any point where $e_1 = e_2$ will serve as an equilibrium. None the less, we can look at the limit point in each instance. Proceeding in this way yields the desired result:

$$\lim_{c \to \infty} e_1^N = \lim_{c \to \infty} e_1^C = \frac{w}{b_1 + b_2}. \qquad (3.29)$$

Finally, note that the intuitive motivation for considering a cooperative type of solution hinged upon the inefficiency of the non-cooperative equilibrium. However, this rationale is valid only when it is reasonable to implement a cooperative outcome, which seems to limit its applicability to the case of small groups. Hence, such an argument may indeed apply to the two-worker group considered above. It may not, however, apply so directly to a larger working group.

The Case of Larger Groups

In principle, it is easy to use the parameterization of (3.7) in the n-agent case, although in practice the results can be hard to interpret. It is simpler, therefore, to place some restriction on $F(b)$, the distribution of disutility of effort parameters in the population of agents. A particularly simple case, which still reveals the effects of group size, is when this population consists of two types of workers.

Assume that, with probability n_i/n, a firm will select a worker of type i, possessing parameter b_i, from the population, and let $i = 1,2$. Then, on the average, a firm will hire n_1 workers with b_1 and n_2 workers with b_2. Consider such a firm, and let its total work force be $n = n_1 + n_2$.

Proceeding exactly as before yields the Nash equilibrium level of effort for any worker of type 1:

$$e_1 = \frac{(b_2 + cn)w}{2[b_1b_2 + (b_1n_1 + b_2n_2)c]}. \tag{3.30}$$

The comparative statics are analogous to the earlier model, with two additions.

First, e_1 is dependent upon the relative composition of the firm:[15]

$$\frac{\partial e_1}{\partial n_1} = \frac{(b_2 - b_1)c^2n_2w}{2[b_1b_2 + (b_1n_1 + b_2n_2)c]^2}$$

$$\{\gtrless\} \, 0 \text{ as } b_1 \{\lessgtr\} \, b_2, \tag{3.31}$$

and, analogously,

$$\frac{\partial e_1}{\partial n_2} = \frac{(b_1 - b_2)(b_2c + n_1c^2)w}{2[b_1b_2 + (b_1n_1 + b_2n_2)c]^2}$$

$$\{\gtrless\} \, 0 \text{ as } b_1 \{\gtrless\} \, b_2. \tag{3.32}$$

Here, (3.31) and (3.32) indicate how the composition of the group, in terms of the two types of workers, affects the effort a worker of

---

[15] I assume that n_i can be treated as a continuous variable, whereas in fact a firm employs an integral number of workers. A justification is that, for large enough groups, the error in the approximation is small.

type 1 supplies. For (3.31), if $b_2 > b_1$, an increase in the number of similar type 1 workers raises e_1, as the pressure to conform to the lower production levels of the type 2 workers is diluted, and conversely for $b_2 < b_1$. Exactly analogous logic − diluting or strengthening the effects of group pressure − reveals the signs displayed by (3.32).

Second, the effects of increasing the group size, while keeping the relative size of the two groups constant, can be assessed:

$$\frac{\partial e_1}{\partial n}\bigg|_{(n_1/n_2)} = \frac{(n_2/n)cb_2(b_1 - b_2)w}{2[b_1b_2 + (b_1n_1 + b_2n_2)c]^2}$$

$$\{\gtrless\} \ 0 \ \text{as} \ b_1 \ \{\gtrless\} \ b_2. \tag{3.33}$$

Thus, a larger group, with the same relative composition, implies higher output from the less productive group of workers and lower output from the more productive group. In effect, a result of (3.7) is that a larger group provides more people to whom agent *i* can conform.

We can also look at the total output of the group, $E = n_1e_1 + n_2e_2$. Adjusting for group size by examining average output, $\bar{e} = E/n$, then, given a constant composition of the group.

$$\frac{\partial \bar{e}}{\partial n}\bigg|_{(n_1/n_2)} = \frac{-n_1n_2c(b_1 - b_2)^2w}{2n^2[b_1b_2 + (b_1n_1 + b_2n_2)c]^2} \leqslant 0, \tag{3.34}$$

with equality only when $b_1 = b_2$. From (3.31), we know that increased group size reduces the distance between the e_i. Now it can be seen that, overall, the higher producers reduce their output by more than the lower producers increase theirs, leading to (3.34).[16] Clearly, this result relies on an equiproportionate movement, upward and downward, which is characteristic of the quadratic specification. As such, its generality is unclear.

---

[16] Analogously, $\partial E/\partial c \leqslant 0$, with equality only when there is no heterogeneity in the group. In both cases, increasing the degree of conformity or increasing the number of people in the group (and thus, by (3.7), the number of people to whom an agent can conform) produces a decline in average output.

Heterogeneous Abilities

The final extension to be considered is that of heterogeneous abilities. As with abitrary group size, it turns out that there is, in principle, no difficulty in extending the model quite generally in this manner. It is easier, however, to illustrate some consequences in a simple example.

Perhaps the easiest modification of the basic model is simply to alter the production function so that

$$q_i = a_i e_i \qquad (3.35)$$

where a_i, a multiplicative parameter that relates the ith agent's effort to his or her output, represents i's ability. Then, maintaining the earlier assumption solely for convenience, a firm hires two workers with parameters (a_i, b_i), $i = 1,2$. In this context, as in the basic model above, it is assumed that workers care about conformity with respect to output levels. Hence, i selects e_i so as to maximize (3.7).

With this change, the non-cooperative Nash equilibrium becomes

$$e_1 = \frac{(a_1 b_2 + 2 a_1 a_2^2 c) w}{2 [b_1 b_2 + (b_1 a_2^2 + b_2 a_1^2) c]} \qquad (3.36)$$

which nests the earlier solution (3.9) as the special case when $a_1 = a_2 = 1$. Aside from the complications introduced by the ability parameters, much of the structure embodied in (3.36) is as before. Thus, agent 1's effort is linearly increasing in the piece rate and is decreasing in both b_1 and b_2.

However, there are some additional features that result from the interaction of the ability parameters and the disutility of effort parameters. In general, these render the sign of $\partial e_1 / \partial a_1$ and $\partial e_1 / \partial a_2$ ambiguous, and there seems no easy interpretation of these slopes. A condition is available, however, in assessing the effect of differing levels of conformity:

$$\frac{\partial e_1}{\partial c} = \frac{a_1 b_2 (a_2^2 b_1 - a_1^2 b_2) w}{2 [b_1 b_2 + (b_1 a_2^2 + b_2 a_1^2) c]^2}$$

$$\{ \gtreqless \} \, 0 \text{ as } (a_2/a_1)^2 \{ \gtreqless \} (b_2/b_1). \qquad (3.37)$$

Thus, the slope of effort supply with respect to the degree of conformity now depends upon the interaction of two sets of parameters. If $a_1 = a_2 = 1$, (3.37) would be positive for $b_1 > b_2$, the usual case. If $b_1 = b_2 = b$, then the condition for positivity of $\partial e_1/\partial c$ would be $a_2 > a_1$: with identical disutility of effort parameters, e_2 would exceed e_1 only if $a_2 > a_1$, and in this instance a higher level of c would be associated with a higher level of e_1 in equilibrium. In the general case, the two effects interact to produce the condition (3.37) above.

Conclusion

In relation to the evidence discussed in chapter 2, two questions have been answered. The first of these was the Hawthorne puzzle, and the trivial resolution consisted merely of recognizing the role of conformity. More generally, I proposed a framework for the economic analysis of social influence, and gave an illustration of a model of this type, addressing in a simple way the idea of conformism in workplace behaviour. The nature of such an economic theory was analysed, and some examples of the interaction between social influence and strategic economic motives were presented.

A limitation of this analysis is that, while several of the real-world examples of conformism were essentially dynamic and temporal in nature, the theory in this chapter is exclusively static. Since precedent and the history of a group often seem to be important aspects of actual behaviour, this is an important omission, and in the next chapter, I shall develop a temporal model designed precisely to address these issues.

4

Tradition

The range of examples that have been marshalled, together with many others that the reader might call to mind, suggests something of the generality, perhaps even the ubiquity, of social influence. In many circumstances, such social processes are crucially temporal. Precedent can play a central role; and often a person's status within a group, depending as it might upon the history of that group, can affect which agents are, in the sociologist's terms, 'respected others' from the perspective of a new group member. In this way, the temporal structure of a particular social setting can affect who conforms to whom, and hence may be a critical factor in the overall determination of individual actions. Such a view was certainly present in much of the discussion in chapter 2: the Bennington freshmen conformed to the seniors, the green soldier adapted to emulate the veterans' behaviour patterns, and so on. To adapt the adage a little, 'When (newly) in Rome, do as the Romans do.'

In this chapter I shall develop an economic model of tradition, based upon the idea of conformism. By a tradition I mean a pattern of behaviour, a belief, or a practice, that persists through time as a result of normative social pressure. Two features of this definition are crucial. First, the tradition must be more than a characteristic of one agent, or of one group of agents: it must be a characteristic shared by a sequence of agents, through a sequence of generations. Second, this intergenerational persistence of behaviour must be the result of social pressures, and not merely an artefact of many generations facing, say, the same material opportunities. In relation to my earlier model, the former characteristic of the definition constitutes the innovation, since the essence of the conformism

model can still be used to characterize the social aspect of traditional behaviour. Yet, as will be seen, the temporal structure of the
tradition model is quite a standard one, from the economist's
perspective and, relative to previous economic work, it is the
representation of social influence that is the key.

Before proceeding, it is useful briefly to relate this approach to
some previous work on tradition conducted by sociologists and
social psychologists. In a recent book, the sociologist Edward Shils
wrote:

> Tradition is thus far more than the statistically frequent recurrence
> over a succession of generations of similar beliefs, practices, institu-
> tions, and works. The recurrence is a consequence of normative
> consequences − sometimes the normative intention − of presenta-
> tion and of acceptance of the tradition as normative. It is this
> normative transmission which links the generations of the dead with
> the generations of the living in the constitution of a society. [Shils
> 1981: 24]

Thus, in Shils' view, it is the social aspect of an intergenerational
similarity among actions that is the hallmark of a tradition. My
model gives a particular structure to this social influence, and
demonstrates in a simple way how such an intergenerational
transmission of behaviour patterns could be effected. In the social
psychology literature, too, tradition can play a central role; the way
in which new entrants in a given situation are socialized into the
group is an important topic of study. Child socialization is a
primary example of such a process (see, e.g., Jones and Gerard
1967, ch. 3). Owing to the temporal nature of such matters, it tends
to be rather difficult to design social psychology experiments to
isolate the factors involved in the persistence of traditions, but
much *in situ* evidence has been examined with this aim in mind.

Finally, it is again worth noting that industrial psychologists and
others have focused upon such processes in workplace situations.
Indeed, in one standard text in the field, the very definition of the
working group embodies this idea of tradition: 'a group is a social
system, composed of two or more members playing different roles
and interacting with each other in such a way that old members can
leave and new ones enter, and yet the system can be identified as the
same' (Smith 1964: 150). The purpose of this chapter, which I

regard as complementary to these various works in other disciplines, is to give a theoretical structure to this idea of tradition, and to analyse some of the consequences for behaviour that thereby arise.

A Model of Tradition

The model that I shall construct follows the precedent established in the previous chapter, in that I shall examine traditions of behaviour within the context of a workplace. As before, I adopt this strategy both because this example has an inherent interest and because of the economy of modelling given by such specificity. The model employed has many singular features, most of which are present merely for expository ease. The critical features of the theory will be remarked upon in the presentation that follows. In view of the similarity between parts of this model and that of chapter 3, I give its assumptions quite briefly.

Sequential Hiring and Overlapping Generations

Owing to high costs associated with separations of employer and employee, resulting from, for example, the loss of specific human capital, training expenses, and losses of morale consequent upon high labour turnover, I shall consider a model with sequential hiring of labour. Thus, a new worker is not hired by a complete re-shuffling of the labour force across firms: rather, the new worker is a piecemeal addition to the existing labour pool at a given firm. This is the temporal analogue of the assumption in the previous model that reassignment of workers among firms was prohibitively expensive. Clearly, this is just a limiting case of the more general idea that such reallocations are costly, to some degree, and the results derived under the assumption that these costs are very large evidently carry over to this more general case. Paralleling our earlier remarks, it seems that, almost without exception, such sequential hiring is a characteristic common to many firms.

The natural treatment of such sequential hiring in a temporal context is through a model of overlapping generations. It will be through conformism between neighbouring generations that we generate traditions passed down from one generation to the next. Moreover, it is worth noting at this point that nothing of significance hinges upon the discrete nature of these overlapping groups. A theory that involved some continuity in the initiation and termination of employer–employee relationships, perhaps of a probabilistic nature, would essentially result in the same mechanism for the intertemporal transmission of traditions. The generational structure merely makes such a social process explicit.

Behaviour of Firms

Competitive firms produce homogeneous output q using labour inputs, and we adopt the simplest production function

$$q_i = e_i \tag{4.1}$$

where q_i and e_i are worker i's output and effort, respectively. The firms can sell all they wish at a fixed price p, this being invariant through time. As before, they pay a constant fixed cost, T, per employee in each period, and their variable costs, depending upon output, are based on a pure piece rate, w; this rate is determined endogenously in each period by the condition that a potential entrant should expect to make zero profits.

I assume that each firm employs workers of two generations, the 'young' and the 'old', except in the first period when it employs only young workers. For ease of exposition, I will fix the group size at 2: this is completely inessential to the results that follow. Thus, a firm employs one member of each generation, and, in the context of sequential hiring, it retains its young employee from one period to become its old employee in the next.

Information in the Labour Market

Workers are heterogeneous in tastes – their disutility of effort parameters, b_i – but homogeneous in ability. It is assumed that, when each firm selects its young employee, it does not know the tastes of the newly hired worker; rather, it merely makes a random draw from the population of workers, $F(b)$, and then, given sequential hiring, it retains this worker from youth to old age. Each generation is characterized by such a distribution, $F(b)$, and these are assumed to be invariant through time.

The rationale for this assumption is that, as before, some degree of heterogeneity in the workforce is needed for conformism to have any role. This extreme assumption could be weakened in a number of ways, of course, without losing the essence of the results. The firms could, for instance, infer possibly incomplete information about worker types, possibly at a cost, and possibly imperfectly. I neglect this issue at present, both because others have worked this ground and for simplicity in modelling.

Behaviour of Workers

Each worker lives for two periods, during which he or she is, respectively, young and old. Since in the model it is assumed that only one worker of each generation is hired by a typical firm, it is convenient to label the workers according to their order of hiring, with worker i being hired upon the death of worker $i - 2$.

When young, we assume that workers act in a manner similar to that in the model of chapter 3. That is, each acts so as to maximize

$$U^i = we_i - b_i e_i^2 - c(e_i - e_{i-1})^2 \qquad (4.2)$$

by choice of e_i. The first two terms represent the utility of wage income and the disutility of effort, in the usual way, while the third represents the desire of the young worker i to conform to the 'respected other', worker $i - 1$.

There are many possible assumptions concerning the behaviour of the workers when old. On the one hand, it might be thought sensible to treat both young and old identically, in which case it would be natural to have each old worker maximize an appropriately re-labelled version of (4.2). On the other hand, the motivation for such conformism − a desire to be like the 'respected other' − need not be identical for the young and the old. In this view, although workers within a generation are presumed to behave in the same way, it might be sensible to assume that, other things being equal, differential status within the group produces differential behaviour patterns. For example, the old workers might not conform at all to the young if, from an 'old' perspective, the young do not qualify as respected others. Or perhaps the old would conform, but to a lesser degree.

Of the social psychological studies detailed in chapter 2, those with an explicitly temporal nature − paralleling the structure of the present overlapping-generations model — seem to support the idea that, while the young conform to the old, the old need not necessarily reciprocate this conformity. For example, Newcomb's study of Bennington College detailed how the young generation, the 'conservative freshmen', conformed to the behaviour of the respected others, the 'liberal seniors' of the old generation. Similarly, in the evidence from *The American Soldier* (Stouffer et al. 1949, vols I and II), it was the replacement — the young placed in a group of old veterans — who conformed, while the veterans themselves were left unaffected by the presence of the green troops. Thus, a difference in status can confer a difference in attitudes about conformism, and it seems right that the model should reflect this fact.

Given this, my strategy is as follows. I shall initially examine behaviour under the supposition that members of the old generation do not conform to the actions of the young. Rather, I assume that the old maintain their behaviour as it had been in the preceding time period, when they were young. This idea — that the workers internalize the behaviour pattern they pursued when young — is critical to the theory, since it is this mechanism that creates the linkage between effort levels in neighbouring time-periods. (Since it is so central, and since it also has an independent interest, I devote chapter 5 to a study of this phenomenon, taking the tradition model one step further to generate a model of value internalization in a process of socialization.) Finally in this chapter, I also consider the other benchmark case, in which the young and the old conform equally to one another.[1] This does not produce traditions, but it does yield a particular type of interdependence of workers' actions, an interdependence that might, for example, be crucial in hiring decisions.

---

[1] A characterization of innovation, rather than tradition, could even involve the old conforming to the young, but not vice versa. The young bring in new ideas or practices, and the old then adapt to these advances. For example, Kuhn (1963) suggested that new scientific ideas are typically produced by new entrants into the discipline; and, similarly, many technological innovations come not from within an industry, but from outside (e.g. Mansfield 1968), despite the apparent head-start of those already familiar with the subject. For one reason why this advantage of the 'old' might only be apparent, based on Festinger's (1957) theory of cognitive dissonance, see Akerlof and Dickens (1982).

Sequential Solution of the Model

In the first period, a typical firm hires agent 1 to work alone, and in this instance I take the third term of (4.2) to be zero. Hence, the maximization of worker 1's quadratic utility function yields

$$e_1 = \frac{w}{2b_1}. \qquad (4.3)$$

Here, as throughout this analysis, w is endogenously determined in equilibrium, with an expected zero profit condition implying that

$$w^* = p - \frac{T}{\int \bar{e} dG(\bar{e})} \qquad (4.4)$$

where $G(\bar{e})$ is the distribution of average output levels across all firms, corresponding to the distribution of workers' tastes, $F(b)$; and thus $\int \bar{e} dG(\bar{e})$ is the average output in the economy as a whole. Since p, T, and $F(b)$ are invariant through time, it follows that, by considering a large enough economy so that the distributional pairings of b_i do not matter overall, w^* is also constant over time: a calculation, which is omitted, reveals that this is true even allowing for the unusual nature of the initial, start-up period.

In the second period, the typical firm hires agent 2, who constitutes the young generation in the firm. Thus, according to the assumptions above, this agent (correctly![2]) takes e_1 as given − the old worker's behaviour is left unaffected by the entry of the new blood − and maximizes a utility function of the form (4.2) to yield

$$e_2 = \frac{(b_1 + c)w}{2b_1(b_2 + c)}. \qquad (4.5)$$

Thus, although worker 1 did not conform to worker 2, the younger worker did conform to the old, with

$$\frac{\partial e_2}{\partial b_1} \leqslant 0. \qquad (4.6)$$

---

[2] The correctness of worker 2's presumption as to the fixity of e_1 contrasts with the familiar 'right for the wrong reasons' characterization of Nash conjectures.

As such, the structure of the model is, in this one-sided manner, quite analogous to the treatment in chapter 3.

The real structure of the model emerges, however, when worker 1 dies and worker 3 is hired. By the terms of the tradition model, e_2 is left unaffected, while worker 3 maximizes (4.2) to yield

$$e_3 = \frac{[b_1(b_2 + c) + c(b_1 + c)]w}{2b_1(b_2 + c)(b_3 + c)}. \tag{4.7}$$

The model is one of tradition, and not just static conformity, in the following sense: even though worker 1 has died, his or her 'dead hand' still lives on. That is, directly from (4.7),

$$\frac{\partial e_3}{\partial b_1} \leqslant 0 \tag{4.8}$$

with strict equality only when $c = 0$, the degenerate case. Hence, even though workers 1 and 3 never worked together, worker 1's disutility of effort parameter affects worker 3's optimal choice of effort level. The mediation, of course, is done by worker 2, who, as a novitiate, conformed to e_1, and who, as an elder statesperson, was himself or herself conformed to by worker 3. It is for this reason that it can be called a model of tradition.

It is informative briefly to consider a graphical representation of this type of process (see figure 4.1). In the upper left-hand graph, worker 1's 'reaction function'[3] is simply a vertical line at the value $w/2b_1$ as given by (4.3). Given this, worker 2's reaction function, $e_2(e_1)$, is upward-sloping, and the equilibrium level of e_2 clearly depends on the past decision of worker 1, as is characteristic of the conformism model.

In the next period, e_2 remains unchanged at the level given by (4.5), so, in the upper right-hand graph worker 2's 'reaction function' is just a horizontal line. The young worker in this context, worker 3, has a reaction function $e_3(e_2)$, yielding the equilibrium value shown in the graph and given analytically by (4.7). The tradition aspect of the model is then readily seen. Had b_1 been lower, e_1

---

[3] Strictly speaking, as e_1 is predetermined before generation 2 is hired — and similarly for e_j before worker $(j + 1)$ enters the scene — there is only a degenerate reaction function, the vertical line in the upper left-hand graph.

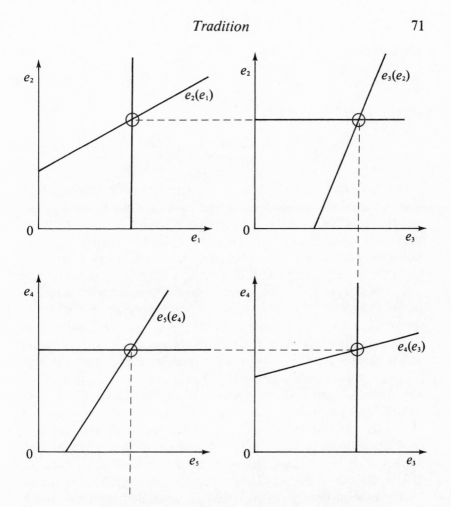

FIGURE 4.1 The intergenerational transmission of tradition. The circles denote equilibrium points.

would have been higher, and the equilibrium in the upper left-hand graph would have involved a higher value of e_2; in turn, this value for e_2, transferred over to the upper right-hand graph, would have yielded a higher value of e_3. Furthermore, this process can be continued, moving to the lower right-hand graph and then the lower left-hand graph, and so on, and the socially based dependence of e_4, e_5, ..., upon the decisions of past generations is evident.

If this process is continued for an arbitrary number of periods, a backward recursion yields an expression for the effort level of the *j*th generation worker, for $j \geqslant 2$:

$$e_j = \left[\sum_{k=0}^{j-2} \frac{1}{c} \prod_{i=0}^{k} \left(\frac{c}{b_{j-i} + c} \right) \right.$$

$$\left. + \frac{1}{b_1} \prod_{i=0}^{j-2} \left(\frac{c}{b_{j-i} + c} \right) \right] \frac{w}{2}. \qquad (4.9)$$

This expression is informative since it permits an explanation of the role of 'the past' in a general type of setting. On the one hand, it shows that *any* e_j depends, to a degree, upon *all* of the past b_i: the past is always with us, to some extent. On the other hand, it reveals how this dependence of e_j on b_i, for $j > i$, declines as $j - i$ increases, since the weights are products of terms each of which is less than unity. In fact, this rate of decline depends precisely on the slopes of the various reaction functions, since the kth generation worker has a reaction function with slope of $c/(b_k + c)$, and each product in (4.9) is simply made up of these terms. Hence, in relation to figure 4.1, it can be seen that, tracing the dependence of e_5 back through b_4, b_3, b_2, and b_1, this dependence consists exactly of the product of the slopes of the various reaction functions. In particular, for generation k, as b_k becomes larger, the slope of the reaction function $e_k(e_k - 1)$ is smaller, and the degree to which a tradition is transferred from generation $k - 1$ to generation $k + 1$, through worker k, is less.[4] Thus, although one might be able to trace the effects of the founding fathers of the group, their influence decreases with time − in an intuitively sensible manner − and is zero in the limit.[5]

It may also be informative to detail some numerical examples illustrating this dependence, and three very simple cases are given in table 4.1. In each instance, the workers' effort levels are listed per unit of the piece rate: as w is constant through time, given by (4.4), we can let it equal unity with no loss of generality. Two sets of effort

---

[4] This statement is valid when e_k is measured on the vertical axis, as is the case for even-numbered generations in figure 4.1. For odd-numbered generations, the larger is b_k, the steeper is the reaction function.

[5] We can also note that (4.9) is sensible in a mathematical sense. To see this, let b_j^- and b_j^+ denote the infimum and the supremum, respectively, of the sequence $\{b_i\}_{i \geq 1}$. Then, noting

levels are detailed, one corresponding to the case of 'isolation', where $c = 0$, and one corresponding to the 'group' case, where the value of c is given in the table. In other words, the former effort levels are just $1/2b_i$, since $w = 1$, while the latter levels of effort are found from (4.9). In case (a) the effects of hiring a below-average output worker in generation 2 are illustrated. Owing to the high standard set by worker 1, e_2 is about 28 per cent higher in the group context than it would have been had agent 2 worked in isolation. In subsequent periods, however, future workers supply less effort in the group than they would have in isolation, although by the tenth generation this effect has declined to a reduction of less than 1 per cent.

In case (b) an opposite situation is illustrated, with unusually

---

that

$$\left(\frac{c}{b\bar{\jmath} + c}\right)^{k+1} \geqslant \prod_{i=0}^{k} \left(\frac{c}{b_{j-i} + c}\right) \geqslant \left(\frac{c}{b\ddagger_j + c}\right)^{k+1},$$

and defining

$$e(b\bar{\jmath}) = \left[\sum_{k=0}^{j-2} \frac{1}{c} \left(\frac{c}{b\bar{\jmath} + c}\right)^{k+1} + \frac{1}{b_1} \left(\frac{c}{b\bar{\jmath} + c}\right)^{j-1}\right] \frac{w}{2}$$

and $e(b\ddagger_j)$ analogously, it follows that, for $j \geqslant 2$,

$$e(b\bar{\jmath}) \geqslant e_j \geqslant e(b\ddagger_j).$$

Thus, the effort that worker j supplies is bounded by expressions that depend upon the infimum and the supremum of the sequence of disutility of effort parameters recorded at j's firm. Moreover, in the limit,

$$\lim_{j \to \infty} e(b\bar{\jmath}) = \frac{w}{2b^-}$$

where $b^- = \lim_{j \to \infty} b\bar{\jmath}$, and analogously for $e(b\ddagger_j)$, so that

$$\frac{w}{2b^-} \geqslant \lim_{j \to \infty} e_j \geqslant \frac{w}{2b^+}.$$

Thus, the limiting bounds are simply the effort levels corresponding to the infimum and the supremum of the sequence $\{b_i\}_{i=1}^{\infty}$, utilizing a quadratic utility function. That is, if $b_i = b^-$ for all i (in which case $b^- = b^+$, of course), then the third term in (4.2) would always be zero: each agent would be maximizing the same quadratic utility function, and, denoting the constant value of b_i as b, it would follow that $e_j = w/2b$ for all j. Excluding this event, which would occur with zero probability for nondegenerate $F(b)$, the two inequalities above would be strict.

TABLE 4.1

Generation i	b_i	e_i: isolation	e_i: group ($c = 4$)
Case (a)			
1	2.0	0.250	0.250
2	3.0	0.167	0.214
3	2.0	0.250	0.226
4	2.0	0.250	0.234
5	2.0	0.250	0.239
6	2.0	0.250	0.242
7	2.0	0.250	0.244
8	2.0	0.250	0.246
9	2.0	0.250	0.247
10	2.0	0.250	0.248
Case (b)			
1	2.0	0.250	0.250
2	1.0	0.500	0.300
3	1.0	0.500	0.340
4	2.0	0.250	0.310
5	2.0	0.250	0.289
6	2.0	0.250	0.276
7	2.0	0.250	0.267
8	2.0	0.250	0.261
9	2.0	0.250	0.257
10	2.0	0.250	0.254
Case (c)			
1	2.0	0.250	0.250
2	2.1	0.238	0.246
3	2.2	0.227	0.239
4	2.3	0.217	0.231
5	2.4	0.208	0.223
6	2.5	0.200	0.214
7	2.6	0.192	0.206
8	2.7	0.185	0.197
9	2.8	0.179	0.190
10	2.9	0.172	0.182

productive workers being hired in both the second and third generations. Owing to agent 2's conformity to e_1, e_2 is lower in the group situation, compared with the isolation value, by 40 per cent, and this effect persists into the next generation, even though workers 2 and 3 are both identical high-producers, with e_3 being reduced by 32 per cent. Thereafter, of course, the effect of group pressures goes the other way, as the influence of the second and third generations lives on after them, though by the tenth round the gain in output owing to this good working tradition has declined to less than 2 per cent.

Finally, in case (c) a situation is simulated whereby the sequence of b_i is increasing over time. In the case of isolation, this clearly results in a declining sequence of effort levels, a natural result of increasing disutilities of effort. The decline is also evident in the group output case, but, owing to the dependence, the rate of decay is lessened: in effect, the effort levels in the group context lag the decline of the isolation values by an average of more than a generation.

There are many ways in which the present model could be extended, both analytically and with further numerical examples. Firms could hire more workers in each generation, and one could model social pressures in both growing and declining firms. These hirings could be based on information about some worker characteristics; and the length of a worker's tenure at a firm, rather than simply being a lifetime, could be endogenously determined. Numerous other possibilities obviously exist.

It seems, however, that the basic idea would remain the same even in much more complicated models. Moreover, it is worth stressing that this basic structure has much in common with the informal insights of sociologists who have studied tradition, with the complementarity of the two approaches being apparent. To cite Shils once again,

The cohesion of a society is ordinarily conceived of as a feature of a particular movement in time; it is the cohesion of its living members with each other. The older living members help to induct the younger living members into the beliefs and patterns which they have inherited from those who went before them. In this way, the dead are influential, exercising what critics of traditionality have called the 'dead hand of the past'. They are object of attachment,

but what is more significant is that their works and the norms contained in their practices influence the actions of subsequent generations to whom they are unknown. The normativeness of tradition is
the inertial force which holds society in a given form over time.
[Shils 1981: 24–5]

Consequences of the Tradition Model

In this section I shall sketch a number of consequences of the tradition model, illustrating how the basic structure that it embodies can
be used in a variety of areas.

Puzzling Production Functions

It has often been observed that, using apparently quite similar inputs, different firms can have rather different levels of output. In a
study of productivity levels of multinational firms with plants in
both Britain and the United States, for example, Pratten (1976)
recorded that productivity was higher in the US plants by an
average of about 50 per cent. Marglin has noted how, in two cotton
textile mills with identical capital equipment, workers in the northern
Yugoslavian mill tended four times as many machines as workers in
the southern Yugoslavian plant (cited in Akerlof 1981: 42). And, of
course, such an observation provided one of the critical elements
underlying Leibenstein's (1976) theory of 'X-efficiency'.

There are a number of standard explanations of such
phenomena, of course. The most obvious of these is simply that,
since capital and other non-labour factors of production are
sometimes difficult to measure, variations in labour productivity
can, at least in part, be seen as a reflection of the mismeasurement
of these other inputs. Such an explanation probably accounts for a
fair part of Pratten's results, for example, as well as being central in
some recent analysis of the apparent slowdown in productivity
growth in the advanced economies. Of course, though potentially
important in this latter context, such an approach based upon
mismeasurement explains the 'production function puzzle' simply
by explaining it away.

Other approaches hinge upon changes in the efficiency of labour within firms. Prominent among these is the idea of specific human capital (e.g. Parsons 1972; Becker 1975), in which workers change in their effectiveness, typically becoming more efficient, with longer tenure at the firm. Finally, one can explain such puzzles in the production function by Leibenstein's concept of 'X-efficiency'.

The tradition model offers a new view of these observations, based on the idea of changing labour efficiency within a firm as a consequence of that firm's traditions. The idea is straightforward. Suppose there are two identical workers, α and β, each characterized by, say, a disutility of effort parameter of b_i. Suppose, further, that these workers are placed in 'identical' firms, in two senses. First, each firm offers the same material opportunities, summarized by the technology (4.1) and the piece rate, w^*, given by (4.4). Second, each agent α and β is in a working group in which the other group member has a disutility of effort parameter of b_{i-1}. Further, there are no other inputs that could be mismeasured. In this setting, which corresponds exactly to the model of the previous section, of course, inspection of (4.9) reveals that α and β will have the same outputs, e_α and e_β, if the past histories of their working groups, $\{b^\alpha_{i-2}, b^\alpha_{i-3}, \ldots\}$ and $\{b^\beta_{i-2}, b^\beta_{i-3}, \ldots\}$, happen to be identical, or if – by pure chance – these past histories are different but exactly offsetting. If the distribution of tastes, $F(b)$, is nondegenerate, this happens with zero probability, so that, although α and β are identical, and although the situations are quite similar, they will almost certainly have different levels of productivity.

Relative to each of the standard explanations, this tradition based rationale constitutes an innovation. It does not rely upon the existence of other, possibly mismeasured, inputs. It is not based upon any changes in the efficiency with which α and β work during their tenure at the firm, since e_α and e_β are constant during the two periods in which they are at their respective firms. Lastly, the tradition result is derived from maximizing behaviour in equilibrium.

There is one qualification to this explanation which is by way of a footnote to the purported 'similarity' of the two working situations. This is that, although both α and β had an identical fellow worker, in the sense that $b^\alpha_{i-1} = b^\beta_{i-1}$, none the less, for different histories of the working groups in the two firms, $e^\alpha_{i-1} \neq e^\beta_{i-1}$. The different 'social environments' at the two firms, to the extent that they affect e_α and e_β, do so through affecting their respective previous generations at the two firms. Thus, if one measured the 'similarity' of their two firms by discovering w^*, b_{i-1}^{α}, and b_{i-1}^{β}, the puzzle of the differences in output between α and β would be explained by the tradition model. However, if one measured this 'similarity' by recording w^*, e_{i-1}^{α}, and e_{i-1}^{β}, then the puzzle would be explained away by this difference in e_{i-1}^{α} and e_{i-1}^{β}. In either case, then, a resolution of the puzzle could arise as a direct and simple consequence of the tradition model.

Finally, we note two points. First, the fact that, with identical technologies and piece rates, $b_{i-1}^{\alpha} = b_{i-1}^{\beta}$ but $e_{i-1}^{\alpha} \neq e_{i-1}^{\beta}$, is, in principle, a testable implication of this model. Second, the model introduces a persistence in the pattern of output levels relative to tastes: agent α and his or her senior in the firm share the same history, $\{b_{i-2}^{\alpha}, b_{i-3}^{\alpha}, \ldots\}$, so one would expect their behaviour, relative to their disutility of effort parameters, to show a similar pattern, as (4.9) reveals. This concept of a working tradition within a firm, which appears to be novel compared with the standard explanations, is the focus of the second implication of the model, to which I now turn.

Good Working Traditions

The preceding analysis described how, with identical technologies, firms employing identical agents could none the less have different levels of output as a result of differing work group histories. This section notes an implication of this fact in equilibrium, which is that, through competitive pressures, a firm must as a consequence seek to engender a 'good working tradition' in its work group.

The theoretical idea is simple. If a firm employs n_j workers in period j – comprised of members of the jth and the $(j-1)$th generations – then, in the model above, it has profits given by

$$\Pi_j = (p - w^*)n_j\bar{e}_j - n_jT \qquad (4.10)$$

where its average output level in period j is $\bar{e}_j$. Hence, using the expression (4.4) for w^*, it follows that, taking w^* as given,

$$\frac{\partial \Pi_j}{\partial \bar{e}_j} = \frac{n_jT}{\int \bar{e}dG(\bar{e})} > 0 \qquad (4.11)$$

so that, in equilibrium, competitive forces will necessitate that a firm seek to maximize $\bar{e}_j$ by, among other things, trying to develop a good tradition of output. The importance of this effect can best be seen by consideration of a particular instance, the case of the Nissan Motor Manufacturing Company USA plant in Smyrna, Tennessee (Shinoff 1983).

The Nissan plant at Smyrna will be the largest venture by a foreign manufacturer in the United States. The plant, set on 825 acres about 15 miles south-east of Nashville, will have its own power plant and test track, and when production reaches planned capacity it will employ 2650 people and produce 156,000 vehicles a year. Overall, the complex will have cost about $500 million to build. Given this huge capital outlay, it is the hiring and labour policies of Nissan that are of particular interest. It can be seen that, to a remarkable degree, these policies could be explained by a concern to establish a good working tradition.

Rather than rely on an existing, skilled labour force, with set traditions and customs, Nissan decided to begin with a comparatively unskilled, new labour force. Initially attracting over 100,000 job applications, Nissan selected workers very carefully, sometimes after as many as 17 interviews and tests. Of those selected, 425, many of whom had never left Tennessee before, were trained, over a considerable length of time and at considerable expense, at a Nissan plant near Tokyo. These workers were to be the 'core' of the labour force, the senior employees, to whom the others would conform, and from whom the others would take their lead.

Since this initial training of the core 425, Nissan then hired 1011 factory and technical employees, gradually building the labour force towards the eventual 2650, full-capacity figure. Furthermore, during this whole period of about a year, no vehicles were produced for commercial sale. Rather, emphasizing once again the role of establishing a good tradition from the outset, this long period was used solely for training and for the development of quality output. By 20 February 1983, only 23 trucks had been built, all of which had been taken apart and checked for defects: 6 of these 23 were then sent to Japan for further testing. In all, it was planned that, by the time production for commercial sale would have begun in August 1983, Nissan would have spent about $173 million on training and salary expenses.

It seems that one could infer the role of tradition in three aspects of this case. First, to the extent that the core 425 workers conformed to the tradition in the Nissan, Tokyo, plant, it was present in the initial training. Second, by using the strategy of a 'core' labour force, whose members had been carefully selected and trained, Nissan had sought to inculcate a high-output, quality-output tradition in the next round of employees, through conformity. Third, to the extent that attrition ensues in subsequent years, when the plant will be operating fully, the old generation of workers will display a high-output norm to the young generation replacements, furthering the good working tradition long after the initial training effects wear off. Given the enormous $173 million outlay on training, one can only infer that this intergenerational aspect of a working tradition is expected to be important. In sum, then, the case of Nissan in Tennessee is a clear, practical example of the role of tradition in a labour force. It illustrates the importance attributed to such phenomena by some managements − paralleling the views of Ouchi cited above (see p. 21) − and it shows in a dramatic way the extent to which a firm can try to achieve a good working tradition, even at a very high initial cost.

Growth Rates of Firms

A final example concerns the implications of the tradition model for the sorting of heterogeneous workers among firms with different rates of growth. The intuition of the result is straightforward. Since highly productive workers will generate more upward conformity in a faster growing firm than in a slow growing one, an equilibrium sorting, however achieved, will be characterized by faster growing firms initially hiring the more productive workers. This result holds in the absence of fixed costs, and in their presence is naturally strengthened.

To see this result in the simplest manner possible, I can sketch an example based upon my earlier model. Consider two firms, A and B. At $t = 1$, each firm hires one worker. At $t = 2$, firm A hires one more worker, retaining its old employee, whereas firm B hires two new workers, also retaining its old employee. Thus, firm B is the faster growing firm, as reflected by its second-period hirings.

Suppose that, at $t = 1$, two workers are available, characterized by b_X and b_Y. Clearly, total output at $t = 1$ is independent of the sorting. However, total output at $t = 2$ depends on the sorting that occurred at $t = 1$. If we suppose that every worker hired at $t = 2$ has a disutility of effort parameter of b_2, then it follows that

$$E_A^2(X) = \frac{(b_2 + b_X + 2c)w}{2b_X(b_2 + c)} \tag{4.12}$$

and

$$E_B^2(X) = \frac{(b_2 + 2b_X + 3c)w}{2b_X(b_2 + c)} \tag{4.13}$$

where $E_j^2(X)$ denotes the total output at firm j $(j = A, B)$ at $t = 2$ if firm j hired X at $t = 1$. Analogous expressions hold for $E_A^2(Y)$ and $E_B^2(Y)$.

Using these formulae, we find that

$$E_A^2(Y) + E_B^2(X) \{ \gtreqless \} E_A^2(X) + E_B^2(Y)$$

$$<=> \quad b_Y \{ \gtreqless \} b_X. \tag{4.14}$$

That is, output is maximized by the faster growing firm, firm B, hiring the more productive worker initially. Hence, under this configuration wages can be higher, given zero profits, than under the alternative sorting.

Of course, although I have derived a sorting in equilibrium, I have not been explicit about the mechanism through which this configuration is reached. To supply this process would require an explicit introduction of the acquisition of information by a firm, whereas, in the model above, an 'extreme ignorance' assumption was made, under which a firm could do no better than make random draws from $F(b)$. Thus, this remains an area where, using the types of sorting mechanisms developed in, for example, Guasch and Weiss (1980, 1982), further investigation is warranted.

Sequential Interdependent Hiring Without Tradition

In this chapter I have developed a model of sequential hiring of labour under the asymmetric assumption that, while the young workers conformed to the behaviour of the old, the old members of the group merely maintained their actions as they had been in the preceding period, when they themselves were young. This assumption, in an overlapping-generations context, gave rise to a model of normative tradition. It was argued there that many social psychological studies, especially those *in situ* in a temporal setting, supported this special assumption.

The purpose of this section is to examine the case in which this assumed generational asymmetry with respect to conformity is relaxed. I do this for reasons beyond a mere desire for intellectual completeness, since there are many situations in which, for one reason or another, members of the old generation do indeed feel pressure, in the socially normative sense outlined in chapter 2, to conform to the young. The processes involved in any real situation are necessarily very complex; and, since they evidently admit of a good deal of variety, it is important to examine the model without the particular 'one-sided conformism' assumption. In many cases, for example, it might be plausible that, depending upon the perceived status of the old generation – the extent to which they are 'respected' by the young, and the extent to which they feel the need of the social approval of the young – the young and old would exhibit differing positive degrees of conformity. The point relevant for this section, however, need not depend upon the precise degrees of conformity involved. Rather, it suffices to characterize the process of sequential hiring in general terms, so that no particular assumption is required, other than the initial one that, at least to some small degree, the old change their behaviour when the young workers enter.

My objective is to show the nature of sequential hiring decisions when there is conformism by both the young and the old. Since the idea is quite straightforward, it suffices to give a verbal account. If the basic structure from above is maintained, letting the degree of conformity be independent of status, then in the initial period worker 1 is hired to work alone. In the next period worker 2 is hired, and by a process analogous to that in chapter 3, both workers 1 and 2 conform to one another. As in the tradition model, the output of worker 2 will depend on the social environment in which he or she is placed. However, unlike that model, the entry of the new blood also produces a change in the actions of the established worker, who now comprises the old generation. That is, the entry of worker 2 in effect alters worker 1's social environment, and the output that worker 1 produces is affected as a result. Hence, in addition to assessing the expected value of worker 2's own contribution to profits, the prudent firm must also assess the effect of his or her entry into the working group, evaluating the extent to which the output of worker 1 alters as a consequence of the change in 1's social environment.

Of course, as the output of existing workers changes, the wages they receive may also change. In one circumstance such changes will be exactly offsetting, in terms of the firm's profits; this is the case in which wages exactly adjust to changes in the value of output, keeping a zero profit condition in each period. As a consequence, although complicated social processes may be present, our prudent firm can carry on, heedless of such niceties, provided the fixed cost T is zero.[6]

Except for this case, however, the interdependence of old and new employees' output levels will be important. It is typically argued in the economic literature that, if the acceptance wages of the unemployed are sufficiently flexible, then they will all be hired. The present theory, however, reveals that, in addition, one would need some flexibility in the wages of the currently employed, since hiring a new worker would also affect *their* output levels. If, for example, most wages have a degree of short-run rigidity – reflecting long-run productivity levels, perhaps, but not changing in response to transitory factors – then, even if the unemployed are prepared to work at any positive wage, it is possible that firms would not be willing to employ them. A low-output worker might not be hired, not because his or her own output is negative, but because, even when paid a very low wage, such a worker could induce conformist declines of output by the existing labour force.[7]

---

[6]   For a positive fixed cost T, of course, competitive pressures will force firms to maximize average output – spreading the fixed cost as broadly as possible – so that, even when wages fully adjust to changes in output, the firm will be compelled to care about the effect of such social interdependencies on the output of its existing employees.

[7]   Note that such a qualitative conclusion can be reached in other ways, given other assumptions. For example, if there were technological interdependencies, such as in a team production process, a similar result could hold, even if the wage paid to the low-output worker were perfectly flexible. Or, if there were a fixity in the number of jobs, as in Akerlof (1981), a low-output worker could 'waste' the resource of the job itself, a resource that could better be used by a more productive worker, so that the low-output worker might not be hired, even at a zero wage. The present result, which holds without assuming any technological interdependence or any such fixity, is thus complementary to these other approaches.

Clearly, such a theory has implications both for the existence of unemployment and for its incidence.

This section has offered a straightforward gloss on a very familiar theory, based on the idea of a socially rooted inter-dependence of output levels within a working group. The gloss is that, even if the wages of those seeking employment are not sticky at all, under some conditions the usual results can hold. However, some degree of rigidity in the wages of the currently employed is still needed: to this end, the usual arguments – perhaps I should say the traditional arguments – can be invoked.

Conclusion

I have presented a theoretical structure for the economic analysis of tradition, using the example of generations of workers within a firm deciding how much effort to supply. But, clearly, such a structure could apply in many other situations. Allport, in his classic study of the nature of prejudice, advanced the conjecture that 'about a half of all prejudiced attitudes are based only on the need to conform to custom, to let well enough alone, to maintain the cultural pattern' (1954: 286), and he presented a careful and insightful discussion of how attitudes and prejudices might be transmitted from parent to child (see especially his chs 17–20). In a discussion of the *esprit de corps*, Schelling noted that many colleges, fraternities, and military units are 'social organisms that are subject to a substantial rate of replacement but that maintain their own peculiar identities to an extent that does not seem to be accounted for by selective or biased recruitment' (1960: 92). Indeed, he cited cases where the legal iden-tity of an army division is maintained even when its numbers are quite minimal, the apparent idea being that the traditions associated with the unit are worth maintaining, should a future in-crease in numbers ever prove necessary. In this instance, traditions can persist, even if the numbers involved in the overlapping genera-tions are very small. And other examples, such as traditions within a particular faculty or department, readily come to mind. Manifestly, our theory of tradition is not limited to the workplace.

Of course, as noted above, the structure of the tradition model hinges upon there being a difference in conformism depending upon the status of the person within the group. Such a difference can be firmly grounded in the idea of the internalization of values, and in the next chapter I shall make this idea, and its underlying social psychology, explicit.

5

The Internalization of Values

A critical assumption of the preceding chapter was that, when 'old', agents maintained their behaviour as it had been in the previous period, when they were 'young'. It was this assumption that enabled the link to be made between effort levels in neighbouring periods. When coupled with the conformity of the young to the old, the model then yielded equilibrium effort levels dependent, in an economically intuitive way, upon the behaviour of all preceding generations: that is, it yielded traditions in equilibrium.

The purpose of this chapter is to take such an idea one step further, developing an explicit model of the 'internalization' of attitudes, values, and past behavioural patterns. An important advance in the social psychology literature on conformity, and actually more generally with regard to many types of social pressure, has been the recognition that conclusions can be reached concerning the persistence of such social influence. Transitory compliance can exist in some circumstances, while quite fundamental changes in values can result in others, with a wide range of intermediate responses to such social pressure also being possible. Furthermore, and perhaps most important, actions that begin as somewhat disingenuous compliance − going along with the crowd with regard to political attitudes, for example − can eventually lead to changes in attitudes that involve a complete alteration of a person's worldview. Of course, the complexities of such a process are immense, and I do not pretend to be able to tackle all of the many subtleties associated with such changes. Rather, complementary to the insights of social psychologists and others, I give a simple analytical characterization in an attempt to highlight some of the key elements involved.

In relation to the economics literature, this chapter can be seen as proposing a new view of endogenous preferences. Previously, models have been constructed whereby, as a consequence of habit or addiction effects, present actions reflect past behaviour in an intuitive manner (see, e.g., Gorman 1967, Peston 1967, Pollak, 1970, 1976a, von Weizsäcker 1971, El-Safty 1976a, 1976b, and Hammond 1976b).[1] In addition, and dating at least from Veblen (1899), economists have characterized some types of interdependent preferences – the bandwagon and snob effects, and so on (see, e.g., Leibenstein 1950 and Pollak 1976b). The present approach complements these insights by joining the concepts of social pressure and internalization in a particular manner. As will be seen, this approach yields new implications, applicable in a variety of areas. Moreover, to a degree that is perhaps unusual in economics, I employ the findings of formal social psychology when developing the model.

Finally, relative to past work in economics, a third area of research is noted, nascent in comparison with the other two, which is closely related to the ideas in this chapter. The essence of this literature is that loyalties can play a central role in affecting behaviour, and Hirschman (1970) is perhaps the seminal work, at least in modern times. Such ideas were extended by Akerlof (1983b), where models incorporating value-changing experiences – 'loyalty filters', in his terminology – were capable of explaining class and institutional affiliations and loyalties. The focus in that treatment was on how agents' choices among experiences are altered if the agents are aware of potential changes in their values as a consequence of these choices. My model is complementary to this research, since it provides a clear and explicit characterization of how, in fact, such changes in values could occur.[2]

---

[1] In related work, Stigler and Becker (1977) have argued that, to the extent that past behaviour affects current actions, it does so in the context of stable preferences. In this view, an agent's past exposure to music enables a growth of that agent's 'music capital', so that, even with given tastes, the agent listens to more music in the future. Or, to cite another example, 'addiction to heroin – a growth in use with exposure – is the *result* of an inelastic demand for heroin, *not*, as commonly argued, the *cause* of an inelastic demand' (1977: 81; italics in original).

[2] In a later work, Hirschman (1982) presents a fascinating account of 'shifting involvements' between private and public goals, based upon affiliations and loyalties that change through experiences.

My strategy is as follows. I shall first review some of the social psychological literature relating to internalization, setting the terms, so to speak, for the subsequent analysis. I shall then build a model of such processes, analogous to the earlier theory of tradition, revealing how value-changing experiences can affect actions and characterizing the interpersonal and intergenerational dependence of behaviour that results. Some comparisons with the existing economic literature on endogenous preferences are presented, particularly with a view to drawing an empirical distinction among these various hypotheses. Finally, I shall assess the broader implications of the tradition-cum-internalization theory, both for economics and also for social analysis, more generally interpreted.

Social Psychology and Internalization

The discussion of conformism in chapter 2 was focused upon two particular issues: the generality of such social influence, and the extent to which such behaviour could be distinguished from the results of strategic economic considerations. A consequence of this emphasis, however, is that some of the subtle social psychological distinctions made among various types of conformism were slurred over. For the most part, I shall maintain this interdisciplinary division of labour in this section; the interested reader is referred to, for example, Aronson (1980, ch. 2) and the references therein for a more extended discussion and analysis. However, it is important for the present purpose briefly to assess the nature of and the inter-relationships among various types of conformism, thereby establishing the characteristics of the process that subsequently will be modelled.

As was indicated above, it seems sensible to envisage a range of possible responses to social influence. With regard to conformism, there seem to be two possible interpretations of this kind of spectrum. One could simply categorize such behaviour according to how close the resulting actions are, relative to how distant the actions would be in the absence of such social forces: in terms of the basic model in chapter 3, this merely amounts to assessing the magnitude of the conformity parameter, c. An alternative interpretation, which I think more interesting, focuses upon the extent to which the conformism results in more fundamental changes in attitudes, and it is upon this view of the diversity of conformist responses that I shall concentrate.

A useful classification of potential responses to social influence was developed by Kelman (1961). Though readily applied to many social processes, it is simplest to illustrate his trichotomy with regard to conformism. The three ideas upon which he focused were compliance, identification, and internalization. Compliance amounts to a straightforward response to social pressure: if social rewards potentially accrue from, say, conforming to some standard, then a compliant response can ensure these benefits. In particular, it should be noted, such a response says little about the underlying attitudes of the agent who complies with regard to the action in question.[3] In a similar way, identification is not crucially linked to the action actually taken: rather, it refers to the desire by one person to be like another, to emulate the 'respected other'. Thus, identification occurs when one person admires another, and when conformity results as a consequence of a wish to define one's self-image as being like this other person.

Finally, and distinct from the other two responses, internalization arises when an agent actually conforms because of a personal attitude about the action: 'it is the content of the induced behaviour that is intrinsically rewarding ...' (Kelman 1961: 65). Moreover, such a response is, in an important sense, more fundamental than either compliance or identification. As Aronson wrote, 'The internalization of a value or belief is the most permanent, most deeply rooted response to social influence. Once it is part of our own system, it becomes independent of its source and will become extremely resistant to change' (1980: 30). Thus, internalization refers to the aspect of the process of socialization through which attitudes, values, and behaviour patterns come to be maintained,

---

[3] It does reveal something, of course. An utterly repugnant action would not be undertaken, even if such a refusal would amount to non-compliance. More generally, the subject would offset the personal utility costs of taking the compliant action, at the margin, against the social costs incurred by any non-compliance, precisely as illustrated in the model of chapter 3.

even in the absence of external rewards or punishments.[4] There are many examples of such 'persisting motives', of patterns of behaviour that are sustained even when their original rationale has been removed. Here, I shall mention just a few that illustrate the potential importance of the subject.

In a classic example, Merton (1968) studied dysfunctional behaviour of bureaucrats, whereby values such as discipline and formalism, originally conceived to produce specific operational results, became aims in and of themselves. Appropriate attitudes in one circumstance became internalized, and were applied even when inappropriate: 'There occurs the familiar process of *displacement of goals* whereby "an instrumental value becomes a terminal value"' (1968: 253; italics in original).[5]

In another example, Allport noted how, although a sailor might have originally gone to sea for the money, he remained a sailor having internalized a 'love of the sea'. In Allport's terms, a 'functional autonomy of motives' led to such persistence, even when the original primary reinforcer was no longer dominant (1937: ch. 7).

Taking a broader view, but one consistent with much of social psychology, it could be argued that child socialization represents the most pervasive example of internalization. According to this position, children receive external reinforcements, both punishments and rewards, that condition their behaviour. As the child becomes socialized these reinforcements cease to be present; nevertheless, through internalization, the behavioural traits that the rewards and punishments had once supported tend to persist (see, e.g., Jones and Gerard 1967: ch. 3 and the references contained therein). In a similar vein, Durkheim wrote as follows,

---

[4] Internalization is a key element in such a process. As defined by Jones and Gerard, socialization refers to 'the adoption and internalization by individuals of values, beliefs, and ways of perceiving the world that are shared by a group' (1967: 76). The reader is referred to their discussion for a treatment of the subtle interrelation between internalization and socialization.

[5] Note one potential qualification to this particular piece of evidence. In such an organizational structure, the incentives the bureaucrats faced might be precisely those that encouraged such behaviour. In a way, much recent economic research in incentives – the principal–agent problem, and so on – can be seen as an attempt at understanding incentives in teams and businesses. Unfortunately, it does not seem possible to infer if such an incentive-based theory suffices in an analysis of Merton's evidence. I conjecture that such a rationale might provide part, but not all, of a complete answer.

speaking about social pressures and constraints:

> If, in time, this constraint ceases to be felt, it is because it gradually gives rise to habits and to internal tendencies that render constraint unnecessary; but nevertheless it is not abolished, for it is still the source from which these habits were derived ... This unremitting pressure to which the child is subjected is the very pressure of the social milieu which tends to fashion him in its own image, and of which parents and teachers are merely the representatives and intermediaries. [Durkheim 1938: 6]

Finally, it is interesting to note how such ideas of internalization were present in our earlier evidence. In Newcomb's study at Bennington College, the students as seniors maintained their behavioural tendency to be liberal, as learned when they had been freshmen: the evidence cited above (p. 26) provides a clear insight into such internalization. Similarly, in *The American Soldier* study Stouffer et al. 1949, vols I and II) the 'green' soldiers maintained the attitudes shown to them by the more senior troops when they themselves become veterans.

Thus, from the evidence detailed here, as well as extensive evidence elsewhere,[6] it appears clear that internalization is an important phenomenon. However, the reason *why* people internalize values and behavioural patterns is less obvious. A traditional interpretation was that, having learned a response, an agent would not easily perceive a change in external circumstances. It hinged, therefore, on the agent's inability to distinguish between 'conditions of learning' and 'conditions of extinction' (McClelland 1951).

An alternative view, based in part on the idea of cognitive dissonance (Festinger 1957), was advanced by Lawrence and Festinger (1962). According to this argument, people would seek to *justify* their efforts: 'if a person ... expends effort that is not readily justified by the amount of reinforcements received, he tends to create reinforcements out of the stimuli available in the immediate surrounding environment ...' (Jones and Gerard 1967: 89). This concept of 'effort justification', which a large number of studies have documented (e.g. Aronson and Mills 1959, Festinger and

---

[6] Homans (1951) contains many other examples of how groups can effect long-lasting changes in the behaviour of their members.

Carlsmith 1959, and Lawrence and Festinger 1962), can provide a basis for internalization. Although the action may have become dysfunctional, it is maintained, and, through effort justification, the dissonance between the effort expended and the minimal reinforcements received is resolved.[7]

A Model of Internalization

In this section I shall develop a simple model of internalization and conformity in the labour market. The structure resembles that of the two previous chapters, with one important difference: in the present model workers move from firm to firm — and from work group to work group — and thus undergo a sequence of different work experiences. Each of these working groups in turn provides a different context for conformity; and, through the internalization of the behaviour patterns produced by past conformity, the actions of a worker depend, in an economically sensible way, upon the work experiences to which he or she has been exposed.

Assumptions

Since many of the details of the model are by now familiar, I merely list the assumptions in summary fashion. Perfectly competitive firms each produce output q using labour effort e according to the trivial production function, $q_i = e_i$, where i indexes the (heterogeneous) workers, and total output at a firm employing n workers is $\Sigma_{i=1}^{n} e_i$. Output can be sold without limit at price p, and firms pay a pure piece rate w, determined endogenously in equilibrium, so that worker i receives a wage of $W_i = we_i$. In addition, firms face a fixed cost T per employee in each period, and the equilibrium difference between p and w^* reflects this cost T and the average output taken across all firms in the economy, $\int \bar{e} dG(\bar{e})$. I maintain the assumption that $n = 2$ solely for expository convenience.

The novelty of the model is twofold. First, workers undergo a

---

[7] A related paper that treats another aspect of cognitive dissonance, and that may be viewed as modelling another type of value-changing experience, is Akerlof and Dickens (1982).

variety of work experiences, moving from firm to firm. Second, in response to this, they act so as to internalize their past behaviour patterns.

The former assumption can be motivated in many ways. In the sequential solution detailed below, it is easier to assume that, after each period, all workers re-enter the labour pool, from which each firm then makes two random draws: these two workers will constitute its workforce for the subsequent period. However, this type of structure would also be consistent with more complex models, where separations of employer and employee, either layoffs or quits, were partial, random, overlapping, or even endogenous. Since we will keep track of only one typical worker, it does not matter, except for technicalities,[8] that we assume a complete turnover of the entire labour force at the end of each period.[9]

The latter assumption – that of internalization – is central. Its precise formulation, and its implications, are given in the sequential solution below.

Finally, before proceeding with this solution, it is appropriate to note the relationship between this model and that of the previous chapter. In the tradition model of chapter 4, an agent was seen as conforming when young, and then, having internalized this pattern of behaviour, was seen as maintaining the same behaviour when old. Here, however, I provide a model of a worker who undergoes a sequence of these value-changing experiences. Moreover, whereas the tradition model hinged on the status difference of the young and the old, that distinction is absent in the present model.

In a more complicated setting one could incorporate all of these elements. For brevity and clarity, however, I make the simplest

---

[8] Among these technicalities would be the fact that, if the separations occur in some systematic way, reflecting the characteristics of the workers involved, then the distribution of workers available in each period would not be $F(b)$, but would rather depend upon the characteristics of the workers who were not retained.

[9] If costs are associated with turnover, of course, then a firm would have an incentive to reduce such a rotation of the labour force. However, as nothing of importance hinges upon the assumption of complete turnover – any degree of partial turnover giving the same qualitative results – it is simplest not to dwell upon this aspect of a firm's behaviour. Similarly, provided some heterogeneity remains, one can allow many types of sorting of worker types – testing, self-selection, and so on – without affecting the overall character of one's results.

assumptions at present, so as to highlight the nature of internalization.

Sequential Solution of the Model

In the first period, each worker operates in isolation, and I assume that, in this case, each has a quadratic utility function,

$$U^i = we_i - b_i e_i^2 \qquad (5.1)$$

where, as usual, b_i is the exogenous disutility of effort parameter for agent i: this is the source of the heterogeneity of the labour pool.[10] In this case of isolation, then, worker 1 supplies an effort level given by

$$e_1 = \frac{w}{2b_1}. \qquad (5.2)$$

In the second period, workers 1 and 2 are placed together in a firm, and, with each maximizing a utility function of the form

$$U^i = we_i - b_i e_i^2 - c(e_i - e_j)^2, \qquad (5.3)$$

the non-cooperative Nash equilibrium has

$$e_1(2) = \frac{(b_2 + 2c)w}{2[b_1 b_2 + (b_1 + b_2)c]} \qquad (5.4)$$

where $e_i(j)$ denotes the output of worker i when working in a group of two with worker j. Thus far, all is very familiar.

---

[10] If experiences determine values, at least in part, as the present model suggests, then it might be thought inconsistent to posit a distribution of *initial* exogenous parameters, $F(b)$. To this charge there are two defences. First, in the view of this chapter, both tastes and experiences are jointly involved in producing actions, so there is nothing *a priori* incorrect in beginning with a taste, b_i. Second, one has to start somewhere. As Homans remarked, discussing a similar issue of culture and personality, 'In order, so to speak, to set the group going, we have assumed that individuals have sentiments that they bring to the group from somewhere outside it, but we have not tried to explain why these sentiments, the sentiments that enter the external system, are what they are . . . In a society made up of many groups of different kinds, the process is more complicated, needs created in one group being met in others. Here, the circularity of the process creating and satisfying needs holds only for society as a whole . . .' (Homans 1951: 331). A later discussion, especially on p. 97 below, indicates how, in this model, the initial b_i do indeed become unimportant in the limit.

The innovation of the model now arises in that, having supplied $e_1(2)$ in the second period, we suppose that worker 1 internalizes this behavioural pattern. That is, he or she determines that, were there no external stimulus, which here is the presence of worker 2, he or she would nevertheless maintain an effort level of $e_1(2)$. In terms of the model, this internalization means that, were agent 1 working in isolation, he or she would supply effort equal to $e_1(2)$. Thus, inverting the quadratic solution (5.2) – which worker 1 used in isolation – we find that a disutility of effort parameter of

$$b_1(2) = \frac{w}{2e_1(2)} \tag{5.5}$$

would exactly internalize the effort level $e_1(2)$.[11, 12] Here, $b_i(j)$ is the disutility of effort parameter that internalizes $e_i(j)$, according to (5.1). In terms of the original parameters, we substitute (5.4) into (5.5) to yield

$$b_1(2) = b_1\left(\frac{b_2 + c}{b_2 + 2c}\right) + \frac{b_2c}{b_2 + 2c} \tag{5.6}$$

so that the internalizing parameter, $b_1(2)$, is a linear function of b_1, where both the intercept and the slope depend upon b_2 and c.[13]

---

[11] In terms of the cognitive dissonance interpretation of internalization mentioned above, note that one could define the dissonance of this group decision, $d_1(2)$, as, say,

$$d_1(2) = \left| \frac{w}{2b} - e_1(2) \right|$$

where b is a parameter to be determined. Then, according to this interpretation, agent 1 would seek to minimize this dissonance by choice of b, which clearly yields

$$b^* = \frac{w}{2e_1(2)}$$

which is just $b_1(2)$ in equation (5.5). In this fashion, the process of internalization can be interpreted as a process of minimizing dissonance, appropriately defined.

[12] It is worth noting that, though particularly simple for the quadratic case, such an argument could readily be extended to other instances. All that is required is that, for each i, the relation between e_i and b_i is strictly decreasing, so a higher disutility of effort is associated with a lower supply of effort, and hence a well-defined inverse obtains.

[13] Note that, for $c = 0$, (5.6) implies that $b_1(2) = b_1$, so that the present model nests more standard treatments as a special case.

In the third period a firm hires worker 3, paramaterized by b_3; and worker 1, who, having internalized his or her previous period's behaviour, is paramaterized by $b_1(2)$.[14] With each maximizing a utility function of the form (5.3), the non-cooperative Nash equilibrium is characterized, for agent 1, by

$$e_1(3) = \frac{(b_3 + 2c)w}{2\{b_1(2)b_3 + [b_1(2) + b_3]c\}}. \tag{5.7}$$

Thus, $e_1(3)$ depends not only upon current opportunities and the current social environment for conformity, but also upon the previous experiences of worker 1, as internalized in $b_1(2)$.[15]

In turn, of course, the effort level, $e_1(3)$ is internalized in a similar way to before, so that, inverting the quadratic solution once again,

$$b_1(3) = \frac{w}{2e_1(3)} \tag{5.8}$$

and, analogous to (5.6),

$$b_1(3) = b_1(2)\left(\frac{b_3 + c}{b_3 + 2c}\right) + \frac{b_3c}{b_3 + 2c}. \tag{5.9}$$

In terms of the original parameters,

$$b_1(3) = \left[b_1\left(\frac{b_2 + c}{b_2 + 2c}\right) + \left(\frac{b_2c}{b_2 + 2c}\right)\right]\left(\frac{b_3 + c}{b_3 + 2c}\right) + \left(\frac{b_3c}{b_3 + 2c}\right) \tag{5.10}$$

This expression illustrates how the internalization of a sequence of effort levels, resulting from conformity in a sequence of working

---

[14] In an economy in which all agents are undergoing a variety of employment experiences and, in a similar manner to worker 1, are internalizing the resultant effort levels, one would need to specify b_3 more precisely. Thus, if, in the preceding period, worker 3 had worked in a group with agent 2', producing effort level $e_3(2')$, then his or her internalized disutility of effort parameter would now be $b_3(2')$. For clarity, I choose to neglect this notational issue. It is clear, however, that a more complicated model would have to take this property, and perhaps the property mentioned in n. 8 above, into account.

[15] To reiterate the preceding note, in a more complicated equilibrium $e_1(3)$ would also depend upon the past experiences of worker 3. Since one needs to keep track of only one worker to see the final result in the present context, this detail is omitted for the time being.

groups, produces a particular form of persistence in observed behaviour.

In general, as worker 1 goes from a group containing worker $i - 1$ to a group containing i, he or she undergoes a sequence of actions. First, he or she conforms to $i - 1$, and then internalizes this $e_1(i - 1)$ as $b_1(i - 1)$; then, in the next group he or she conforms to i, and then internalizes this $e_1(i)$ as $b_1(i)$. Thus, the revision in his or her disutility of effort parameter is given by

$$b_1(i) = b_1(i - 1)\left(\frac{b_i + c}{b_i + 2c}\right) + \left(\frac{b_i c}{b_i + 2c}\right). \qquad (5.11)$$

By a backward recursion, similar to that employed in chapter 4, it then follows that, for $i \geqslant 2$,

$$b_1(i) = \sum_{j=0}^{i-2}\left\{\left[\prod_{k=0}^{j-1}\left(\frac{b_{i-k} + c}{b_{i-k} + 2c}\right)\right]\left(\frac{b_{i-j}c}{b_{i-j} + 2c}\right)\right\}$$

$$+ \prod_{j=0}^{i-2}\left(\frac{b_{i-j} + c}{b_{i-j} + 2c}\right)b_1. \qquad (5.12)$$

Expression (5.12) illustrates how, in this specific model, the values that worker 1 embodies depend, in a particular way, upon the work experiences through which he or she has gone. In this stylized setting, conformity to various working group members, coupled with subsequent internalization of the behaviour so produced, yields an expression for an agent's disutility of effort parameter as a function of all past parameters, together with the degree of conformity, c. Since the weight on b_1, agent 1's own disutility of effort parameter in the initial period, is the product of terms, each less than unity for $c > 0$, it follows that, as the number of work experiences becomes large, the importance of b_1 in determining $b_1(i)$ becomes small, and in the limit is zero. In the end, the 'environment' determines everything, although, after any finite number of job transitions, both these experiences and the initial disutility of effort play a role.

Moreover, the pattern of the weights on b_j, for $j = 1, 2, \ldots, i - 1$, is intuitive, with more distant work experiences receiving a smaller role in the determination of $b_1(i)$, as (5.12) reveals. Further, the rate of this decline is affected by the slopes of the reaction functions at each of these firms, so that, the greater is b_j, the smaller is the rate of decline of the weights in period j. Thus, though a little complicated, (5.12) is in fact perfectly in accord with our intuition.[16]

More generally, this simple model provides an explicit treatment of 'value-changing experiences', detailing both the source of the external stimulus to change and the internalization of the resultant action. As was seen in the preceding chapter, such a structure can give rise to traditions of behaviour; and, in the last section of this chapter I shall address the issues raised by this tradition-cum-internalization theory. Before doing this, however, I shall make a brief digression concerning the relation between this view of changing tastes and those approaches typically employed in the economics literature.

Other Approaches to Endogenous Preferences

As was mentioned earlier in this chapter, there have been many other characterizations of endogenous tastes in the economics literature. In comparing the present theory with these earlier models, my intention is not to engage in a thorough survey, but simply to make two points.

The first is that, in my model, preferences might be inconsistent, in the sense that each worker is seen acting myopically in selecting one period's e_i, even though he or she might anticipate that, in the next period, his or her b_i will have altered as a result. This naive strategy contrasts with a sophisticated approach in which, anticipating the future change in tastes, the worker takes this potential change into account in selecting the current e_i.[17] In contrast to some of the existing literature, however, I do not necessarily regard

---

[16] Expression (5.12) also reveals the mathematical properties embodied by the model. A straightforward argument, which I have omitted, analogous to that in n. 5 to chapter 4, establishes bounds on $b_1(i)$ for any finite i, depending on the largest and smallest of these b_i, and, in the limit, shows that

$$b^- \leqslant \lim_{i \to \infty} b_1(i) \leqslant b^+$$

where b^- and b^+ are the infimum and the supremum, respectively, of the sequence $\{b_i\}$.

[17] For a clear discussion of these issues in a more general context, see Hammond (1976a).

such an inconsistency as an undesirable feature of the model. Social influence is external to the agent, in a sense that eating a habit-forming cake is not, and perhaps a positive theory describing such social forces and their influence upon behaviour needs to incorporate such a feature. It is fairly clear, for example, that many people's attitudes about 'the proper role of women' have changed over the past 25 years: should we somehow have anticipated this change, in which social pressures certainly played a part? It seems that demanding consistency may on occasion make our theories lose some of their force.

The second point in relating the present theory to other work on changing tastes concerns how one might draw an empirical distinction among the various hypotheses. Like the other models, the present view of tradition and internalization is a statement about the world, rather than a proposition in logic, so it cannot admit of direct proof. Rather, one must assess its validity, compared with that of its competitors, through observation.

In general terms, such a precise distinction among competing hypotheses is exceedingly difficult. Unless some parametric assumptions are made as to functional form, for instance, the dependence upon past behaviour implied by addiction, by Stigler and Becker's (1977) 'capital' accumulation, and by the tradition and internalization model may be quite similar. Needless to say, the applied worker makes such particular assumptions with great caution.

There are two features of the present model, however, that may allow an empirical distinction to be drawn. First, the *interpersonal* transmission of customs is particular to the notion of conformity. The evidence cited in chapter 2 suggested that this might be an important piece of structure, and hence that it might provide a useful basis for evaluating the various theories. Second, as argued above, the *intergenerational* transfer of traditions is also a particular feature of the present viewpoint, and one that, it was argued, provided broad empirical support for the tradition and internalization position.

More generally, although empirical distinction can be very hard, in a formal sense, this need not blind one to the obvious. Conformity, tradition, and the internalization of values are so manifestly pieces of reality that it makes sense to 'call a spade a spade', and only Veblen's 'trained incapacity' could suggest otherwise.

Some General Implications

Finally, I wish to examine the types of general implications that arise from these twin models of internalization and tradition. Many issues are raised by such theories, of course, and I do not propose to address all or even most of them here. Instead, both because it illustrates what I believe are the central points and for reasons of brevity, I shall focus on one particular question, and discuss the implications of the theory within this context.

The question, which has been a central problem in social research, is: How can it be that, beginning with relatively similar material conditions, societies have developed in such a large number of diverse ways? (See, e.g., Lewis 1976, Harris 1979, and Leach 1982.) To the extent that the customs and traditions of a society are determined by material conditions, with only those customs that contribute best to, say, 'genetic fitness' and 'reproductive success' surviving, the puzzle lies in the apparent similarity of initial material opportunities. On the other hand, to the extent that customs and norms are given more latitude, and need only be 'consistent' with material survival — which, prima facie, all extant customs are, of course — the puzzle lies in developing a rigorous model of how traditions can persist through many generations and how, in addition, such a diversity of traditions could in fact arise.

In a very particular sense, I claim that the present models of internalization and tradition are important in an examination of both of these approaches. They suggest that the former puzzle may be ill-posed, and, on the constructive side, they offer one initial, structural framework for addressing the latter issue.

With regard to the first point, the models can be interpreted as providing a simple counter-example to the strict materialist position. If agents engage in behaviour in accordance with traditions, through the twin processes of conformity and internalization, where adherence to these traditions is sought *per se*, then, except in a world with unchanging material opportunities, these agents will *not* be acting so as best to cope with the material problems that they encounter. Rather, the model introduces a persistence in behaviour so that the customs of today are an accumulation of responses to past circumstances, both social and material. Therefore, to the extent that agents both adhere to past traditions and generate new ones, the naive materialist position is suspect.[18]

Could this conclusion have been derived from a more standard economic model of, say, 'habits', or from (in Stigler and Becker's terms) a model of the accumulation of 'capital'? The answer seems to be no, except in so far as a very particular model of changing opportunities is developed.[19] The reason is that, while the time-scale implicit in the problem posed at the start of this section is long – over many generations – these models both lack this inter-dependence between neighbouring generations, characteristic of the tradition model, which can produce a long-lived intertemporal dependence. Rather, when an agent eating a habit-forming cake dies, the habit also dies. Or, when an agent with a particular accumulation of 'Mozart capital' dies, this stock of 'capital' is lost. Thus, unless it could be argued that yesterday's habits altered today's material opportunities, and altered them in a very special way, the 'one-generational' approach of these two theories distinguishes them from the 'many-generational' model of tradition.

Turning to the constructive aspect of my model, the problem is twofold: first, how traditions can persist through many genera-tions; and second, how such a diversity of traditions can actually arise. As we have seen, the first issue is a problem for standard theory since, without some dependence, one period's idiosyncracies would likely be counterbalanced by the next period's own quirks, and, as independent trials, no persistence would ensue. The answer, in terms of the models of tradition and the internalization of values,

---

[18] The qualifier 'naive' is added since, taking the argument one step back, a 'sophisticated' materialist could question why this 'taste for tradition' arises in the first place. Of course, the social psychology of chapter 2 offered something of an answer to that question, but the debate continues none the less.

[19] A parent's 'stock of Mozart capital' could make it easier for a child to acquire its own stock, thereby producing an intergenerational transmission in the Stigler and Becker (1977) framework. But, clearly, this depends on a special model of how today's behaviour affects later opportunities, and its generality is therefore questionable. One might also wonder whether it or our model of conforming to one's parents' liking for Mozart is a simpler and more natural characterization.

is straightforward, of course, where differences in past behaviour, rather than cancelling out, are maintained and even developed through time. The models provide a detailed, maximizing account of how such a dependence can occur.

The second problem remains, however, in that, although we have generated intertemporal traditions, the limiting behaviour of the system (5.12) is characterized by a unique equilibrium, given a particular sequence of experiences. I conjecture that the explanation of this diversity of customs, given some quite similar material circumstances, must lie in a model of tradition and internalization with multiple equilibria. Integrating the constructive approach of the present treatment with the 'coordination problem' paradigm mentioned in the opening chapter promises to be a challenging task for future work.

6

Conclusion

In this book, I have presented several illustrations of a new class of economic models, the hallmark of these theories being that, while people are still seen as engaging in 'calculating avarice', they are not regarded as being immune from social influence. By characterizing some interpersonal processes as a tendency towards conformism, a simple theory was generated whereby actions are the result of an interaction of preferences, opportunities, and the social environment. In a static context, this produced a model of partial adherence to norms of behaviour in which social pressures both arose from and at the same time impinged upon the decisions of utility-maximizing agents. Intertemporally, such a structure gave rise to an economic theory of tradition and, by an extension of the model, to an analysis of how social forces acting on behaviour could produce changing values and attitudes as a result. A number of consequences were discussed, some particular to the case of workplaces and some having greater generality.

In this brief final chapter I would like to propose a few areas for further investigation, building upon the framework developed above. As before, some of my ideas concern labour market behaviour, while others stray somewhat further from the particular context of the current theories.

With regard to the workplace examples, I noted in an earlier chapter that a rich agenda of research is feasible concerning the interrelationship between various economic incentive structures and the social aspects of behaviour stressed in the present models. One topic that has recently received much attention has been the incentive structures that arise as a result of contests in which, broadly speaking, workers are paid according to their rank relative to others (see, e.g., Lazear and Rosen 1981, Green and Stokey, 1983, Nalebuff and Stiglitz 1983, and O'Keeffe, Viscusi, and Zeckhauser 1984).

In a sense, it is tempting to suggest that such a literature has been too successful, since, by demonstrating that contests may be a desirable form of incentive system under relatively plausible assumptions about information and risk, the theories have generated the new puzzle of why, in fact, contests are not even more prevalent. One conjecture, first advanced, I believe, by Nalebuff and Stiglitz, is that contests necessarily alter the nature of the work environment, so that, in a broader model in which worker effort and morale depend on this social context, contests might have harmful consequences missed in the conventional economic analysis. Hence, akin to some of the extensions of the model presented in chapter 3, one could examine this conjecture in the framework of the conformist approach to such social factors, assessing the nature of the interaction between such economic incentives and social pressures. It might be, for example, that if these sociological concerns do indeed vitiate the advantages of contests, then one would expect to see payment by relative output when social interactions among the competitors are few – travelling salesmen being an obvious example – whereas, when social influence among co-workers is high, other incentive mechanisms, which work with the social incentives and not against them, might be employed. If such a conclusion ensues, then the over-achievement of the contest models would have been valuable, of course, since it would have provided a stimulus towards a closer examination of aspects of workplace behaviour other than purely material incentives. Needless to say, perhaps, I would regard such a result as desirable, although it should be stressed that a serious analytical treatment is needed before such implications can be drawn.

Another extension of the models of workplace behaviour would be to incorporate trade unions into the analysis. One of the most widely expressed concerns about the Hawthorne evidence was that, in examining some sociological factors at the Western Electric Company, the researchers all but ignored the role of unions; and perhaps my theories are open to a similar charge. To a large degree, of course, one would expect social influence to persist with or without unions, and in that sense it may not seem that I have made a fatal omission. None the less, many aspects of the labour market are critically affected by trade unions, and one would clearly like to address such effects in a full account. This promises to be a difficult task, however, since, as I briefly noted in the introductory chapter, most theories of unions have not been grounded in individual behaviour and therefore are rather contrary to the spirit of the present model. Recently, several authors have proposed theories based ultimately on the actions of the union's members (e.g. Oswald 1982, Lazear 1983, and Blair and Crawford 1984), and perhaps eventually this type of theory could be integrated with the present analysis. But clearly this is a project still far from fruition.

In more general terms, a potentially important area for future work concerns models of social behaviour with multiple equilibria. One reason for looking at this, as noted earlier, is that both the 'coordination problem' paradigm and the present theory are somewhat incomplete as full theories of custom and convention. The former approach seems to omit many constructive social processes by which conventions can arise; while the latter, though offering a remedy to this problem, fails to capture the multi-equilibrial nature of many social phenomena. It would be useful to combine these two approaches more precisely. A second reason, closely related to the first, concerns models in which individual rationality generates a socially suboptimal outcome, the 'prisoners' dilemma' being the canonical example. In some circumstances, a desire for conformity may in effect change a prisoners' dilemma game, in material terms, into a game of coordination, in terms of overall utilities; so that pre-play communication, though futile in the case of a prisoners' dilemma, becomes valuable in achieving a socially optimal outcome in the case of coordination. It would be interesting to characterize when such a result is likely to hold, and hence when social pressures can vitiate somewhat destructive economic incentives.

Another area of interest concerns the nature of collective choices. Typically, the economic approach to such issues assumes that social choice is an attempt at combining various individual preferences, something like an aggregation problem, and such work has rigorously analysed the conditions when such a social choice, appropriately defined, can be made.[1] At the same time, some psychologists have sought to study how, in fact, various collectives and groups come to decisions, with a key characteristic being the interdependence of attitudes that can result in such situations.[2] That is, groups, committees, and so on usually make choices as a result of compromises and complicated social interactions within the group: the preferences of one member can affect the positions of the others, thereby producing a consensus where, initially, none existed. It would seem that, by modelling this type of process, the present approach can complement the standard economic analysis in a positive model of group choice.

Finally, I mention one possible application of these theories. A standard assumption in economic models, which I myself followed above, is that people dislike work, at least at the margin. One consequence, emphasized by some writers, is that, to the extent that the overall financial loss associated with unemployment is small, the offsetting utility gain from not having to work can make one question the involuntary nature of such unemployment. To some people, at least, such a conclusion seems implausible, perhaps leading one to doubt the premise that underlies this implication. In addition, of course, we all know of cases where such assumptions about the disutility of work are incorrect, perhaps from our own experience.

One way to address this type of issue is to consider the possibility of socially determined 'norms' of labour supply: there is a social expectation that people will work, so that, as a result, social losses ensue to those who are not able to find employment. This need not imply that, from a personal perspective, people like to work hard, but it does suggest that, for social reasons, people might need the 'category' of a job, 'man's strongest tie to reality' in Freud's (1930) terms. That is, employment provides, among other things, a structure to time, a role and opportunity for shared experiences, a sense of purpose, and a means of acquiring self-identity and status. Analogously, a loss of employment involves a loss of these various

---

[1] Arrow (1951) is the seminal work, of course. For a recent survey of this literature, see Sen (1977).
[2] Some notable examples in this tradition are Allison (1971), Janis (1972), and Kyle (1980).

functions, as well as a reduction in income, and a proper characterization of the nature of unemployment must take these losses into account.

The theories developed above could be used to examine these issues, with a social norm of employment arising endogenously from past employment levels. In this way, the socially determined loss experienced by an unemployed person could depend, for example, on the overall level of unemployment then prevailing. The extent of this loss could vary with the duration of the unemployment spell, with past employment patterns, and so on. Hence, it seems that such issues could be pertinent in an examination of, for example, persistence in labour market behaviour, the discouraged worker syndrome, the private and social costs of unemployment, and the extent and timing of unemployment insurance schemes. A proper examination of these and other issues, building upon the framework developed above, remains an exciting project for future work.

Bibliography

Ackley, Gardner (1983) Commodities and Capital: Prices and Quantities. *American Economic Review* 73: 1–16.

Akerlof, George A. (1970) The Market for 'Lemons': Quality Uncertainty and the Market Mechanism. *Quarterly Journal of Economics* 84: 488–500.

—— (1980) A Theory of Social Custom, of which Unemployment may be One Consequence. *Quarterly Journal of Economics* 95: 749–75.

—— (1981) Jobs as Dam Sites. *Review of Economic Studies* 48: 37–49.

—— (1982) Labor Contracts as Partial Gift Exchange. *Quarterly Journal of Economics* 97: 543–69.

—— (1983a) Discriminatory, Status-based Wages among Tradition-oriented, Stochastically Trading Coconut Producers. Manuscript, Department of Economics, University of California, Berkeley.

—— (1983b) Loyalty Filters. *American Economic Review* 73: 54–63.

Akerlof, George A. and William T. Dickens (1982) The Economic Consequences of Cognitive Dissonance. *American Economic Review* 72: 307–19.

Alchian, Armen A. and Harold Demsetz (1972) Production, Information Costs, and Economic Organization. *American Economic Review* 62: 777–95.

Allison, Graham T. (1971) *Essence of Decision: Explaining the Cuban Missile Crisis*. Boston: Little, Brown.

Allport, F.H. (1920) The Influence of the Group Upon Association and Thought. *Journal of Experimental Psychology* 3: 159–82.

Allport, Gordon W. (1937) *Personality: A Psychological Interpretation*. New York: Holt.

—— (1954) *The Nature of Prejudice* (25th anniversary edn, 1979). Reading, Mass.: Addison-Wesley.

Aronson, Elliot (1980) *The Social Animal* (3rd edn). San Francisco: W.H. Freeman.

Aronson, Elliot and Judson Mills (1959) The Effects of Severity of Initiation on Liking for a Group. *Journal of Abnormal and Social Psychology* 59: 177–81.

Arrow, Kenneth J. (1951) *Social Choice and Individual Values.* New York: John Wiley.

—— (1972) Models of Job Discrimination. In *Racial Discrimination in Economic Life*, ed. A.H. Pascal, 83–102. Lexington, Mass.: D.C. Heath.

—— (1974) Gifts and Exchanges. *Philosophy and Public Affairs* 1: 4; reprinted in *Altruism, Morality and Economic Theory*, ed. E. Phelps. New York: Russell Sage Foundation.

Asch, Solomon E. (1951) Effects of Group Pressure upon the Modification and Distortion of Judgement. In *Groups, Leadership and Men*, ed. M.H. Guetzkow, 117–90. Pittsburgh: Carnegie.

—— (1952) *Social Psychology.* Englewood Cliffs, NJ: Prentice-Hall.

—— (1956) Studies of Independence and Conformity: A Minority of One Against a Unanimous Majority. *Psychological Monographs* 70, no. 9, whole no. 416.

Bach, K.W. (1951) Influence through Social Communication. *Journal of Abnormal and Social Psychology* 46: 9–23.

Barash, David (1979) *Sociobiology: The Whisperings Within.* New York: Harper and Row.

Bass, B.M. and G.V. Barrett (1972) *Man, Work and Organizations.* Chicago: University of Chicago Press.

Becker, Gary S. (1957) *The Economics of Discrimination.* Chicago: University of Chicago Press.

—— (1974) A Theory of Social Interactions. *Journal of Political Economy* 82: 1063–1109.

—— (1975) *Human Capital* (2nd edn). Chicago: University of Chicago Press.

—— (1976) Altruism, Egoism, and Genetic Fitness: Economics and Sociobiology. *Journal of Economic Literature* 14: 817–26.

Belcher, D.W. (1974) *Compensation Administration.* Englewood Cliffs, NJ: Prentice-Hall.

Blair, Douglas H. and David L. Crawford (1984) Labor Union Objectives and Collective Bargaining. *Quarterly Journal of Economics*, forthcoming.

Blake, Robert B. and Jane Srygley Mouton (1981) *Productivity: The Human Side.* New York: Amacom.

Bowles, Samuel (1983) The Production Process in a Competitive Economy: Walrasian, Neo-Hobbesian, and Marxian Models. Manuscript, Department of Economics, University of Massachusetts, Amherst.

Bowles, Samuel, David M. Gordon and Thomas E. Weisskopf (1983) *Beyond the Waste Land: A Democratic Alternative to Economic Decline*. Garden City, New York: Anchor Press Doubleday.

Bresnahan, Timothy F. (1981) Duopoly Models with Consistent Conjectures. *American Economic Review* 71: 934–45.

Brodbeck, May (ed.) (1968) *Readings in the Philosophy of the Social Sciences*. New York: Macmillan.

Burdett, K. and Dale T. Mortensen (1981) Testing For Ability in a Competitive Labor Market. *Journal of Economic Theory* 25: 42–66.

Cass, Eugene Louis and Frederick G. Zimmer (eds) (1975) *Man and Work in Society*. New York: Van Nostrand Reinhold.

Clark, Rodney (1979) *The Japanese Company*. New Haven: Yale University Press.

Cole, Robert E. (1979) *Work, Mobility and Participation: A Comparative Study of American and Japanese Industry*. Berkeley and Los Angeles: University of California Press.

Collard, David (1978) *Altruism and Economy: A Study in Non-Selfish Economics*. Oxford: Martin Robertson.

Deutsch, Morton and Harold B. Gerard (1955) A Study of Normative and Informational Social Influence upon Individual Judgement. *Journal of Abnormal and Social Psychology* 51: 629–36.

Dickson, William J. and F.J. Roethlisberger (1966) *Counseling in an Organization: A Sequel to the Hawthorne Researches*. Boston: Harvard University.

Dore, Ronald (1973) *British Factory – Japanese Factory: The Origins of National Diversity in Industrial Relations*. Berkeley and Los Angeles: University of California Press.

Dunlop, J.T. (1944) *Wage Determination under Trade Unions*. New York: Macmillan.

Durkheim, Emile (1938) *The Rules of Sociological Method* (8th ed), trans. Sarah A. Solovay and John H. Mueller. New York: Free Press.

Eaton, Curtis and William D. White (1983) The Economy of High Wages: An Agency Problem. *Economica* 50: 175–81.

Edwards, Richard (1979) *Contested Terrain: The Transformation of the Workplace in the Twentieth Century*. New York: Basic Books.

El-Safty, A.E. (1976a) Adaptive Behavior, Demand and Preferences. *Journal of Economic Theory* 13: 298–318.

____(1976b) Adaptive Behaviour and the Existence of Weizsäcker's Long-Run Indifference Curves. *Journal of Economic Theory* 13: 319–28.

Festinger, Leon (1957) *A Theory of Cognitive Dissonance*. Evanston, Ill.: Row, Peterson.

Festinger, Leon and J. Merrill Carlsmith (1959) Cognitive Consequences of Forced Compliance. *Journal of Abnormal and Social Psychology* 58: 203–10.

Festinger, Leon and J. Thibaut (1951) Interpersonal Communication in Small Groups. *Journal of Abnormal and Social Psychology* 46: 92–99.

Firth, Raymond (1956) Function. In *Current Anthropology*, ed. William L. Thomas, Jr, 237–58. Chicago: University of Chicago Press.

Freud, Sigmund (1930) *Civilisation and its Discontents*, standard edn, vol. 21. London: Hogarth.

Gerard, Harold B. (1954) The Anchorage of Opinions in Face-to-Face Groups. *Human Relations* 7: 313–26.

_____ (1961) Some Determinants of Self-Evaluation. *Journal of Abnormal and Social Psychology* 62: 288–93.

Gerard, Harold B. and Edward S. Conolley (1972) Conformity. In *Experimental Social Psychology*, ed. C. McClintock, 237–63. New York: Holt, Rinehart and Winston.

Gerard, Harold B. and Charles W. Greenbaum (1962) Attitudes Toward an Agent of Uncertainty Reduction. *Journal of Personality* 30: 485–95.

Giddens, Anthony (1971) *Capitalism and Modern Social Theory.* Cambridge: Cambridge University Press.

Goldberg, Solomon and Ardie Lubin (1958) Influence as a Function of Perceived Judgement Error. *Human Relations* 11: 275–81.

Gordon, Robert J. (1982) Why US Wage and Employment Behaviour Differs from that in Britain and Japan. *Economic Journal* 92: 13–44.

Gorman, W.M. (1967) Tastes, Habits, and Choices. *International Economic Review* 8: 218–22.

Green, Jerry R. and Nancy L. Stokey (1983) A Comparison of Tournaments and Contracts. *Journal of Political Economy* 91: 349–64.

Guasch, J. Luis and Andrew Weiss (1980) Wages as Sorting Mechanisms in Competitive Markets with Asymmetric Information: A Theory of Testing. *Review of Economic Studies* 47: 149–65.

_____ (1982) An Equilibrium Analysis of Wage-Productivity Gaps. *Review of Economic Studies* 49: 485–97.

Hahn, Frank H. (1981) *Money and Inflation.* Oxford: Basil Blackwell.

Hammond, Peter J. (1976a) Changing Tastes and Coherent Dynamic Choice. *Review of Economic Studies* 43: 159–73.

_____ (1976b) Endogenous Tastes and Stable Long-Run Choice. *Journal of Economic Theory* 13: 329–40.

Harris, Marvin (1979) *Cultural Materialism: The Struggle for a Science of Culture.* New York: Random House.

Harsanyi, John C. (1955) Cardinal Welfare, Individualistic Ethics and Interpersonal Comparisons of Utility. *Journal of Political Economy* 63: 309–21.

Hirschman, Albert O. (1970) *Exit, Voice, and Loyalty.* Cambridge, Mass.: Harvard University Press.

——— (1982) *Shifting Involvements: Private Interest and Public Action.* Princeton, NJ: Princeton University Press.

Holmström, Bengt (1982) Moral Hazard in Teams. *Bell Journal of Economics* 13: 324–40.

Homans, George C. (1951) *The Human Group.* London: Routledge and Kegan Paul.

——— (1953) Status Among Clerical Workers. *Human Organization* 12: 5–10.

——— (1954) The Cash Posters. *American Sociological Review* 19: 724–33.

Ishikawa, Tsuneo (1981) The Emulation Effect as a Determinant of Work Motivation (published in Japanese), *Keizaigaku Ronshu* 47: 1, April.

Janis, I.L. (1972) *Victims of Groupthink.* Boston: Houghton Mifflin.

Jones, Edward E. and Harold B. Gerard (1967) *Foundations of Social Psychology.* New York: John Wiley.

Kelman, Herbert C. (1961) Processes of Opinion Change. *Public Opinion Quarterly* 25: 57–78.

Kiesler, Charles A. and Sara B. Kiesler (1969) *Conformity.* Reading, Mass.: Addison-Wesley.

Kuhn, Thomas S. (1963) *The Structure of Scientific Revolutions.* Chicago: University of Chicago Press.

Kyle, Neil John (1980) *Groupthink in Decision Making: Testing for its Existence, Effects, and Prevention.* Vancouver: University of British Columbia.

Laffont, Jean-Jacques (1975) Macroeconomic Constraints, Economic Efficiency and Ethics: an Introduction to Kantian Economics. *Economica* 42: 430–37.

Landsberger, Henry A. (1958) *Hawthorne Revisited: 'Management and the Worker', its Critics, and Developments in Human Relations in Industry.* Ithaca, NY: Cornell University Press.

Landy, F.J. and D.A. Trumbo (1976) *Psychology of Work Behavior.* Homewood, Ill.: Dorsey Press.

Lawrence, D.H. and Leon Festinger (1962) *Deterrents and Reinforcement: The Psychology of Insufficient Reward.* Stanford, Cal.: Stanford University Press.

Lazear, Edward P. (1983) A Competitive Theory of Monopoly Unionism.

American Economic Review 83: 631–43.

Lazear, Edward P. and Sherwin Rosen (1981) Rank-order Tournaments as Optimum Labor Contracts. *Journal of Political Economy* 89: 841–64.

Leach, Edmund R. (1981) Biology and Social Science: Wedding or Rape? *Nature* 291: 267–68.

_____ (1982) *Social Anthropology*. Glasgow: Fontana.

Leibenstein, Harvey (1950) Bandwagon, Snob, and Veblen Effects in the Theory of Consumers' Demand. *Quarterly Journal of Economics* 64: 183–207.

_____ (1976) *Beyond Economic Man: A New Foundation for Microeconomics*. Cambridge, Mass.: Harvard University Press.

_____ (1982) The Prisoners' Dilemma in the Invisible Hand: An Analysis of Intrafirm Productivity. *American Economic Review (Papers and Proceedings)* 72: 92–97.

_____ (1984) The Japanese Management System: An X-Efficiency-Game Theory Analysis. In *The Economic Analysis of the Japanese Firm in Comparative Perspective*, ed. Masahiko Aoki, 331–57. Amsterdam: North-Holland.

Lewis, David K. (1969) *Convention: A Philosophical Study*. Cambridge, Mass.: Harvard University Press.

Lewis, Ioan M. (1976) *Social Anthropology in Perspective*. Harmondsworth: Penguin.

Lucas, Robert E., Jr (1981) *Studies in Business-Cycle Theory*. Cambridge, Mass.: Massachusetts Institute of Technology Press.

Lumsden, Charles J. and Edward O. Wilson (1981) *Genes, Mind, and Culture: The Coevolutionary Process*. Cambridge, Mass.: Harvard University Press.

McClelland, D.C. (1951) *Personality*. New York: William Sloane.

McCormick, E.J. and J. Tiffin (1974) *Industrial Psychology*. Englewood Cliffs, NJ: Prentice-Hall.

MacDonald, Glenn M. (1980) Person-specific Information in the Labor Market. *Journal of Political Economy* 88: 578–97.

McGregor, Douglas (1960) *The Human Side of Enterprise*. New York: McGraw-Hill.

Mackay, Charles (1852) *Memoirs of Extraordinary Popular Delusions and the Madness of Crowds* (reprinted 1980). New York: Harmony Books.

Maier, N.R.F. (1973) *Psychology in Industrial Organizations*. Boston: Houghton Mifflin.

Malinowski, Bronislaw (1926) Anthropology. *Encyclopaedia Brittanica*

(1st Supplementary Volume). London and New York.

Mansfield, Edwin (1968) *The Economics of Technological Change*. New York: W.W. Norton.

Mausner, Bernard (1954a) The Effect of Prior Reinforcement on the Interaction of Observer Pairs. *Journal of Abnormal and Social Psychology* 49: 65–68.

—— (1954b) Prestige and Social Interaction: The Effect of One Partner's Success in a Related Task on the Interaction of Observer Pairs. *Journal of Abnormal and Social Psychology* 49: 557–60.

Mayo, Elton (1933) *The Human Problems of an Industrial Civilization*. Cambridge: Macmillan.

—— (1945) *The Social Problems of an Industrial Civilization*. Cambridge, Mass.: Harvard University Press.

Merton, Robert K. (1968) *Social Theory and Social Structure* (enlarged edn). New York: Free Press.

Michael, Robert T. and Gary S. Becker (1973) On the New Theory of Consumer Behavior. *Swedish Journal of Economics* 75: 378–96.

Miyazaki, Hajime (1984) Work Norms and Involuntary Unemployment. *Quarterly Journal of Economics*, forthcoming.

Modigliani, Franco and Richard A. Cohn (1979) Inflation, Rational Valuations and the Market. *Financial Analysts Journal* 35: 24–44.

Moore, H.T. (1921) The Comparative Influence of Majority and Expert Opinion. *American Journal of Psychology* 32: 16–20.

Mouton, J.S., R.B. Blake, and J.A. Olmsted (1956) The Relationship Between Frequency of Yielding and the Disclosure of Personal Identity. *Journal of Personality* 24: 339–47.

Nagel, T. (1970) *The Possibility of Altruism*. Oxford: Clarendon Press.

Nalebuff, Barry J. and Joseph E. Stiglitz (1983) Prizes and Incentives: Towards a General Theory of Compensation and Competition. *Bell Journal of Economics* 14: 21–43.

Newcomb, Theodore M. (1943) *Personality and Social Change: Attitude Formation in a Student Community*. New York: Dryden Press.

Newcomb, Theodore M., Kathryn E. Koenig, Richard Flacks, and Donald P. Warwick (1967) *Persistence and Change: Bennington College and Its Students After Twenty-Five Years*. New York: John Wiley.

O'Keeffe, Mary, W. Kip Viscusi, and Richard J. Zeckhauser (1984) Economic Contests: Comparative Reward Schemes. *Journal of Labor Economics* 2: 27–56.

Okun, Arthur M. (1981) *Prices and Quantities: A Macroeconomic Analysis*. Washington DC: Brookings Institution.

Olson, Mancur (1965) *The Logic of Collective Action: Public Goods and the Theory of Groups*. Cambridge, Mass.: Harvard University Press.

Oswald, Andrew J. (1982) The Microeconomic Theory of the Trade Union. *Economic Journal* 92: 576–95.

Ouchi, William G. (1981) *Theory Z: How American Business Can Meet The Japanese Challenge*. New York: Addison-Wesley.

Parsons, Donald O. (1972) Specific Human Capital: An Application to Quit Rates and Layoff Rates. *Journal of Political Economy* 80: 1120–43.

Patten, T.H., Jr (1967) *Pay: Employee Compensation and Incentive Plans*. London: Free Press.

Peston, M.H. (1967) Changing Utility Functions. In *Essays in Mathematical Economics in Honor of Oskar Morgenstern*, ed. Martin Shubik, 223–36. Princeton, NJ: Princeton University Press.

Pollak, Robert A. (1970) Habit Formation and Dynamic Demand Functions. *Journal of Political Economy* 78: 745–63.

—— (1976a) Habit Formation and Long-Run Utility Functions. *Journal of Economic Theory* 13: 272–97.

—— (1976b) Interdependent Preferences. *American Economic Review* 66: 309–20.

Popper, Karl R. (1944) The Poverty of Historicism, II. *Economica* 11: 119–37.

—— (1966) *The Open Society and Its Enemies*, (5th edn, rev.) vol II. Princeton, NJ: Princeton University Press.

Pratten, C.F. (1976) *Labour Productivity Differentials within International Companies*. Cambridge: Cambridge University Press.

Radner, Roy. (1979) Rational Expectations Equilibrium: Generic Existence and the Information Revealed by Prices. *Econometrica* 47: 655–78.

Reder, Melvin W. (1952) The Theory of Union Wage Policy. *Review of Economics and Statistics* 34: 34–45.

Rees, Albert (1962) *The Economics of Trade Unions*. Chicago: University of Chicago Press.

Ribeaux, P. and S.E. Poppleton (1978) *Psychology and Work: An Introduction*. London: Macmillan.

Roethlisberger, F.J. and William J. Dickson (1939) *Management and the Worker*. Cambridge, Mass.: Harvard University Press.

Ross, Lee, Gunter Bierbrauer, and Susan Hoffman (1976) The Role of Attribution Processes in Conformity and Dissent. *American Psychologist* 31: 148–57.

Schachter, Stanley (1951) Deviation, Rejection, and Communication. *Journal of Abnormal and Social Psychology* 46: 190–207.

Schelling, Thomas C. (1960) *The Strategy of Conflict*. Oxford: Oxford University Press.

____ (1978) *Micromotives and Macrobehavior*. New York: W.W. Norton.

Schlicht, Ekkehart (1978) Labor Turnover, Wage Structure and Natural Unemployment. *Zeitschrift für die Gesamte Staatswissenschaft* 134: 337–46.

Schotter, Andrew (1981) *The Economic Theory of Social Institutions*. Cambridge: Cambridge University Press.

Seashore, S.E. (1954) *Group Cohesiveness in the Industrial Work Group*. Ann Arbor: Institute for Social Research, Survey Research Center, University of Michigan.

Sen, Amartya K. (1974) Choice, Orderings and Morality. In *Practical Reason*, ed. S. Korner. Oxford: Basil Blackwell.

____ (1977) Social Choice Theory: A Re-examination. *Econometrica* 45: 53–89.

____ (1979) Informational Analysis of Moral Principles. In *Rational Action*, ed. R. Harrison. Cambridge: Cambridge University Press.

Shapiro, Carl and Joseph E. Stiglitz (1982) Equilibrium Unemployment as a Worker Discipline Device. Woodrow Wilson School of Public and International Affairs, Discussion Papers in Economics, no. 28, April.

Sherif, Muzafer (1935) A Study of Some Social Factors in Perception. *Archives of Psychology*, no. 187.

____ (1936) *The Psychology of Social Norms*. New York: Harper and Brothers.

Shils, Edward (1981) *Tradition*. Chicago: University of Chicago Press.

Shinoff, Paul (1983) Making New Trucks in Tennessee: Why Auto Workers Like Nissan. *San Francisco Examiner*, 20 February, pp. A1 and A26.

Simon, Herbert (1957) *Models of Man*. New York: John Wiley.

Skinner, Andrew (1974) Introduction to *The Wealth of Nations*, by Adam Smith. Harmondsworth: Penguin.

Smith, Adam (1759) *The Theory of Moral Sentiments* (1976 edn), ed. D.D. Raphael and A.L. Macfie. Oxford: Clarendon Press.

____ (1776) *The Wealth of Nations* (reprinted 1974). Harmondsworth: Penguin.

Smith, H.C. (1964) *Psychology of Industrial Behavior* (2nd ed). New York: McGraw-Hill.

Snyder, A., W. Mischel, and B.E. Lott (1960) Value, Information, and Conformity Behavior. *Journal of Personality* 28: 333–41.

Solow, Robert M. (1979a) Alternative Approaches to Macroeconomic Theory: A Partial View. *Canadian Journal of Economics* 12: 339–54.

____ (1979b) Another Possible Source of Wage Stickiness. *Journal of Macroeconomics* 1: 79–82.

____ (1980) On Theories of Unemployment. *American Economic Review* 70: 1–11.

Spence, A. Michael (1974) *Market Signaling: Informational Transfer in Hiring and Related Screening Processes*. Cambridge, Mass.: Harvard University Press.

Stigler, George J. and Gary S. Becker (1977) De Gustibus Non Est Disputandum. *American Economic Review* 67: 76–90.

Stiglitz, Joseph E. (1975) Incentives, Risk and Information: Notes Towards a Theory of Hierarchy. *Bell Journal of Economics* 6: 552–79.

Stoft, Steven (1982) Cheat-Threat Theory. Unpublished PhD Dissertation, University of California, Berkeley.

Stouffer, S.A., E.A. Suchman, L.C. de Vinney, S.A. Star, and R.M. Williams, Jr (1949) *The American Soldier*: vol. I, *Adjustment During Army Life*. Princeton, NJ: Princeton University Press.

Stouffer, S.A., A.A. Lumsdaine, M.H. Lumsdaine, R.M. Williams, Jr., M.B. Smith, I.L. Jarvis, S.A. Star, and L.S. Cottrell, Jr (1949) *The American Soldier*: vol. II, *Combat and its Aftermath*. Princeton, NJ: Princeton University Press.

Sugden, Robert (1982) On the Economics of Philanthropy. *Economic Journal* 92: 341–50.

Swartz, K. (1981) Information in the Hiring Process: A Case Study. *Journal of Economic Behavior and Organization* 2: 71–94.

Ullmann-Margalit, Edna (1977) *The Emergence of Norms*. Oxford: Oxford University Press.

Veblen, Thorstein (1899) *The Theory of the Leisure Class: An Economic Study of Institutions* (1970 edn). London: Unwin Books.

Vickery, W. (1962) One Economist's View of Philanthropy. In *Philosophy and Public Policy*, ed. F.G. Dickinson. New York: National Bureau of Economic Research.

von Weizsäcker, C.C. (1971) Notes on Endogenous Changes of Tastes. *Journal of Economic Theory* 3: 345–72.

Wallich, Henry C. (1979) Radical Revisions of the Distant Future. *Journal of Portfolio Management* 1: 36–38.

White, Michael and Malcolm Trevor (1983) *Under Japanese Management: The Experience of British Workers*. London: Heinemann.

Whitehead, T. North (1938) *The Industrial Worker*. Cambridge, Mass.: Harvard University Press.

Whyte, William F. (1955) *Money and Motivation: An Analysis of Incentives in Industry*. New York: Harper and Row.

Williams, B.J. (1982) Have We a Darwin of Biocultural Evolution? American Anthropologist 84: 848–52.

Wilson, Edward O. (1975) *Sociobiology: The New Synthesis*. Cambridge, Mass.: Harvard University Press.

___ (1978) *On Human Nature*. Cambridge, Mass.: Harvard University Press.

Wintrobe, Ronald (1983) Taxing Altruism. *Economic Inquiry* 21: 255–70.

Index